ASHE Higher Education Report: Volume 40, Nu

Kelly Ward, Lisa E. Wolf-Wendel, Series Editors

Asian Americans in Higher Education: Charting New Realities

Yoon K. Pak

Dina C. Maramba

Xavier J. Hernandez

Asian Americans in Higher Education: Charting New Realities
Yoon K. Pak, Dina C. Maramba, Xavier J. Hernandez
ASHE Higher Education Report: Volume 40, Number 1
Kelly Ward, Lisa E. Wolf-Wendel, Series Editors

Cover image by © Kirsty Pargeter/iStockphoto.

ISSN 1551-6970 electronic   ISSN 1554-6306   ISBN 978-1-118-88490-4

The ASHE Higher Education Report is part of the Jossey-Bass Higher and Adult Education Series and is published six times a year by Wiley Subscription Services, Inc., A Wiley Company, at Jossey-Bass, One Montgomery Street, Suite 1200, San Francisco, California 94104-4594.

Individual subscription rate (in USD): $174 per year US/Can/Mex, $210 rest of world; institutional subscription rate: $327 US, $387 Can/Mex, $438 rest of world. Single copy rate: $29. Electronic only–all regions: $174 individual, $327 institutional; Print & Electronic–US: $192 individual, $376 institutional; Print & Electronic–Canada/Mexico: $192 individual, $436 institutional; Print & Electronic–Rest of World: $228 individual, $487 institutional. See the Back Issue/Subscription Order Form in the back of this volume.

CALL FOR PROPOSALS: Prospective authors are strongly encouraged to contact Kelly Ward (kaward@wsu.edu) or Lisa E. Wolf-Wendel (lwolf@ku.edu). See "About the ASHE Higher Education Report Series" in the back of this volume.

Visit the Jossey-Bass Web site at **www.josseybass.com.**

Printed in the United States of America on acid-free recycled paper.

The ASHE Higher Education Report is indexed in CIJE: Current Index to Journals in Education (ERIC), Education Index/Abstracts (H.W. Wilson), ERIC Database (Education Resources Information Center), Higher Education Abstracts (Claremont Graduate University), IBR & IBZ: International Bibliographies of Periodical Literature (K.G. Saur), and Resources in Education (ERIC).

Advisory Board

The ASHE Higher Education Report Series is sponsored by the Association for the Study of Higher Education (ASHE), which provides an editorial advisory board of ASHE members.

Contents

Executive Summary   vii

Foreword   ix

Acknowledgments   xiii

Introduction   1
Chapter Summaries and Outline   3
Defining "Asian American"   5
Research Literature on Race and Asian America   8
Limitations of the Review and Analysis   11

Historical Overview of the Model Minority Concept   13
Are Asian Americans Considered Racial Minorities in Higher
    Education?   13
The Various Shades of the Yellow Peril   15
The Modern "Model Minority" Emerges   18
The Model Minority Goes to School   22

**Asian Americans and the Educational Pipeline: Tenuous
    Citizenship**   31
Asian American Access to the Educational Pipeline   34
Higher Education and Segregation   38
Asian American Demands for Equal Representation in Higher
    Education   40

Affirmative Action and Asian American Admissions   49
Affirmative Action Defined   49

Affirmative Action Toward the Turn of the Century: (Re)Defining
Merit   52
Negative Action Versus Affirmative Action   56
The Model Minority Goes to Court: The Impact of *Bakke, Gratz,
Grutter,* and *Fisher*   58
Affirmative Action in Contemporary Asian America   61
Potential Implications of the *Fisher* Ruling   67

**Influential Factors in the Asian American and Pacific Islander
College Student Experience**   **69**
Campus Climate   70
Identity Development   73
Family and Intergenerational Concerns   76
Mental Health   78
Leadership and Involvement   81
College Choice   82
Community College   85
The Emergence of Asian American and Native American Pacific
Islander–Serving Institutions (AANAPISIs)   88

Conclusions and Recommendations   **95**
Recommendations for Future Research: Purposeful Disaggregation
of Data   96
Multiracial AAPIs   97
Research Beyond the Model Minority   98
Implications for Policy   98
Implications for Practice   99
Challenges Looming on the Horizon: Conflation of AAPI College
Students and Asian International Undergraduates   101
Concluding Thoughts   105

References   **107**
Name Index   **123**
Subject Index   **129**
About the Authors   **135**

Executive Summary

Diversity is an increasingly important consideration in contemporary American higher education, capturing the attention not only of educators and educational researchers but also legal scholars, politicians, and others. Central to what has resulted broadly as a "diversity rationale" is the belief that educational benefits result from the interaction of heterogeneous student bodies and advance the civic missions of higher education (Gurin, Nagda, & Lopez, 2004; Hurtado, 2007). And although the discourse on diversity includes institutionally transformative potential, it relates significantly still to the preservation of race-conscious policies in admissions to improve the proportional representation of under-represented racial minority students (Chang, 2002; Gurin, Dey, Hurtado, & Gurin, 2002; Museus & Chang, 2009).

The historical and contemporary experiences of Asian Americans in higher education are interesting to consider within this diversity movement. Subject to the persistent stereotype of being "model" minorities whose academic achievement levels have reached parity with or sometimes even surpassed those of Whites and whose presence is characterized as "over-represented" especially in science, technology, engineering, and mathematics (STEM) fields and elite universities, critical scholars have begun to raise the question: Are Asian Americans minorities? To the extent that Asian Americans as a group have been selectively included in measures of campus diversity but also have been deemed ineligible to receive scholarships and other supports designated for minority students, how have institutional policies and practices contributed to the process of "de-minoritizing" Asian Americans? (Lee, 2010; Teranishi, 2010).

In the monograph we engage these queries to challenge the assumed simplicity of "majority" and "minority" racial status and experience, and we underscore the need for focusing attention to equity in discussions of diversity. We consider such matters in light of studies that indicate Asian American students do sometimes face racially hostile campus climates (Cress & Ikeda, 2003) and report lower rates of satisfaction with the college experience than their fellow students (Ancis, Sedlacek, & Mohr, 2000). We explore the growing scholarship in education and other social sciences to better understand the complex nature of Asian American students' experiences. Drawing from quantitative as well as qualitative research, we address how colleges and universities can respond to the immense diversity that can confound approaches to effective delivery of policy and practice.

This monograph will provide educators, administrators, and policymakers who influence all levels of higher education with deeper understanding of how the varied experiences and histories of Asian American students defy facile categorizations. Immigrant and refugee settlement patterns, geographic and regional diversity, language and identity, among others, all serve as critical points to see the contexts for how varied groups of Asian Americans have traversed the K–12 to higher education pipeline. The ways in which Asian American students have access to, or limitations in counseling, financial aid, and other social service needs stem in large part from misunderstandings of the range of Asian American students' experiences. How perceptions of Asian American students have served to mold current practices and policies will be of benefit to both practitioners and researchers in higher education. We aim in this monograph to restructure campus policies related to racial diversity to thoroughly and consistently incorporate Asian Americans as a matter of equity.

Foreword

Asian Americans are often left out of the diversity discussion and agenda in higher education because of assumptions made about their status as "model minorities" and because of assumptions that Asian Americans are not experiencing the same access and climate concerns in higher education experienced by other minoritized individuals. As a result, programs, campus support groups, and policies often either explicitly or implicitly exclude Asian Americans, which can have problematic repercussions for higher education. Part of the problem, as highlighted in this monograph, stems from a failure to disaggregate Asian American students into meaningful groupings. There are a myriad of important differences between and among Asian Americans, some of which are a function of country of origin, reason for immigration, generational status in the United States, and English language proficiency, to name a few. These differences are rarely accounted for individually or as a whole and therefore lead to Asian Americans being overlooked, misunderstood, and narrowly represented in most higher education research and most institutional strategies.

This monograph, *Asian Americans in Higher Education: Charting New Realities* by Yoon K. Pak, Dina C. Maramba, and Xavier J. Hernandez, fills an important void in our understanding of the needs, issues, and concerns facing Asian Americans in higher education. This monograph provides comprehensive information and data about Asian Americans in higher education, culled from a variety of qualitative and quantitative social science sources. The authors tackle such important issues as affirmative action, access to college, campus climate, and what terms like "majority" and "minority" mean in the context of U.S. higher education. This monograph does a great job of providing perspective and advice on how institutions of higher education can better serve, through both policy and practice, the diversity represented within the Asian American community.

This monograph is divided into five chapters—each dealing with an important element necessary to understanding Asian Americans in higher education. The first chapter offers a historical overview of the concept of model minorities and how that relates to the experiences of Asian Americans. The authors argue that the model minority myth has long since framed how Asian Americans are treated in higher education and greatly affects the cultural discourse surrounding this group. The second chapter looks at the educational pipeline, looking specifically for how Asian Americans (disaggregated in meaningful ways) have achieved various educational milestones. This chapter also looks at how colleges and universities have or have not served Asian American student needs. The third chapter looks specifically at admissions policies and affirmative action in relationship to Asian Americans. The authors argue that fear of Asian Americans in higher education, or "yellow peril," is behind much of the rhetoric and actions surrounding admissions policies and decisions. This chapter is especially timely in light of the recent *Fisher v. University of Texas* (2013) Supreme Court case. The fourth chapter looks at the research on the college experience of Asian Americans. In particular, the authors look at the research on the experiences of Asian Americans at four- and two-year institutions and the emergence of special focus colleges with large numbers of Asian American students (called Asian American and Native American Pacific Islander–Serving Institutions [AANAPISIs]). The final chapter offers helpful conclusions related to future research, policy, and practice.

This monograph is a must-read for anyone interested in an array of issues pertaining to Asian Americans and with an interest in achieving an equity agenda in higher education. It will be of use to multiple audiences including college and university administrators, researchers, faculty, graduate students, and anyone interested in Asian Americans in higher education. This monograph pushes readers to think more critically about the context and contributions of Asian Americans in higher education. It clearly makes the point that if we just look at Asian American students as a monolithic group who represents the model minority, we will fail to consider the important and diverse needs of this population.

In the ASHE monograph series as a whole we have been intentional to address issues related to comprehensive understandings about diversity in higher education. Monographs, for example, by Marybeth Walpole on low SES students, by Rachelle Winkle-Wagner on cultural capital, by Amy Lee and her colleagues on engaging diversity in undergraduate classrooms, by Sam Museus and his colleagues on racial and ethnic minority students in STEM, and by Amy Bergeson on college choice and access are complementary to this monograph on Asian American students in higher education. In addition, recent monographs by Anne-Marie Nunez and colleagues on Latinos in higher education, by Eunyoung Kim and her colleagues on immigrant students, and by Bryan Brayboy and his colleagues on Native Americans all focus on the unique situation and circumstances of a particular population while providing a critical and theoretical lens through which to view the success of these student communities. This monograph joins this series to provide a specific focus on Asian Americans.

Acknowledgments

We extend our deepest gratitude to Lisa Wolf-Wendel for lending invaluable support, from beginning to end. Yolanda Davis (PhD student at the University of Illinois at Urbana-Champaign) deftly reproduced all the tables and figures for this project. Robert Teranishi (Morgan and Helen Chu Endowed Professor at UCLA) gratefully gave permission to reproduce all the tables and figures.

The following organizations assisted in the intellectual development and/or funding support of the project:

Education Policy, Organization, and Leadership and the College of Education at the University of Illinois at Urbana-Champaign
Department of Asian American Studies at the University of Illinois, Urbana-Champaign
Association for the Study of Higher Education
American Educational Research Association—Research on the Education of Asian Pacific Americans SIG
Association for Asian American Studies

Last, but not at all least, we give thanks to family, friends, and colleagues who have provided support and encouragement throughout the project.

Published online in Wiley Online Library
(wileyonlinelibrary.com) • DOI: 10.1002/aehe.20013

Introduction

RECENT DEMOGRAPHIC PROJECTIONS by the Western Interstate Commission for Higher Education (WICHE) indicate that Latino/a and Asian American populations will witness the largest increase in growth, particularly in our public secondary schools and in newer regions where population concentrations are beginning to emerge. For example, while public high school graduates of Asian American and Pacific Islander (AAPI) students made up larger proportions of graduating classes along the West Coast, Hawaii, and in some Northeast and Mid-Atlantic states, three eastern states expected to see some of the greatest gains in AAPI population by 2020 are New York, New Jersey, and Virginia, with Texas also witnessing large gains (WICHE, 2012). Along the West Coast, only Washington will add significant numbers by 2020. Although small numerically, Southern and Midwestern states will see higher percentage of projected growth, with Kentucky as a stand out among them (WICHE, 2012). Hawaii, Oregon, and Wisconsin, on the other hand, are forecasted to see negative annual rates of change (WICHE, 2012).

According to the U.S. Census Bureau (2013), Asians were the nation's fastest-growing race or ethnic group in 2012. The population rose by 2.9%, or 530,000 in 2011, to 18.9 million. More than 60% of the growth in the Asian population came from international migration. The combination of growth among Asian and Latino populations, the two highest growing ethnic groups, have contributed to an ever-growing reality of "majority–minority" communities. According to the U.S. Census Bureau (2013) the population of

FIGURE 1

Actual and Projected Proportional Representation of White and Non-White Populations in the United States (1950–2050)

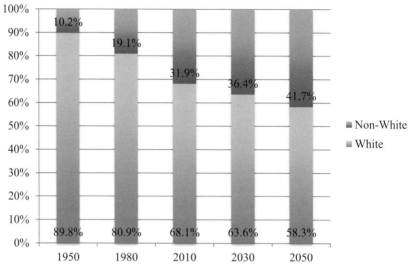

Note: 1950–2010 are actual data; 2030 and 2050 are projected data.
Source: U.S. Census Bureau, Population Division. (2011). From "The Relevance of Asian American and Pacific Islanders in the College Completion Agenda" (p. 5). *The National Commission on Asian American and Pacific Islanders Research in Education.* Adapted with permission.

children younger than five years of age stands to be majority–minority in the near future. As of 2012 that percentage of minority youth stood at 49.9%. The concept of diversity then becomes challenged not only through the shifting population demographics but also in who holds (and will hold) political and social power.

Figure 1 provides an indication of the change, actual and projected, in non-White populations into the middle of the 21st century.

Given these increasing numbers of non-White populations, evaluating the definitions of "minority" and "majority" and whether or not groups still experience discrimination will be paramount. Part and parcel to this debate is the concurrent discussion of how the efforts to reflect the growing diversity of the country throughout the educational pipeline can effectively take place.

Access to education, seen as a fundamental right of American citizenship, has always played a central role in race relations throughout the country's history. Moving forward, debates regarding what exactly the educational system's role should be within society's larger concerns of diversity are prevalent at every level of schooling.

In this monograph, we challenge the assumed simplicity of "majority" and "minority" racial status and experience, and we underscore the need for focusing attention to equity in discussions of diversity. We consider such matters in light of studies that indicate Asian American students often face racially hostile campus climates (Cress & Ikeda, 2003) and report lower rates of satisfaction with the college experience than their fellow students (Ancis et al., 2000). We explore the growing scholarship in education and other social sciences to better understand the complex nature of Asian American students' experiences. Drawing from quantitative as well as qualitative research, we address how colleges and universities can respond to the immense diversity that can confound approaches to policy and practice. We argue at the outset, as the scholars reviewed in this study reveal, that the idea of Asian American overrepresentation needs to be problematized.

Chapter Summaries and Outline

While the concept of the "model minority" existed well before mid-20th century (Ng, Lee, & Pak, 2007), the first chapter, *Historical Overview of the Model Minority Concept*, synthesizes the major publications in popular culture that led to Asian Americans being touted as such. We argue that the model minority framework begins to develop in particular ways for students in secondary and higher education, and that policy measures became adopted to "frame" students in such limited ways. Critical literature on Asian Americans and the model minority is also included to add recent counterpoints to popular culture discourse (Osajima, 1995, 2007; Wu, 2003; Wu & Kidder, 2006).

The second chapter, *Asian Americans and the Educational Pipeline: Tenuous Citizenship*, provides a historical overview of how, when, and under what circumstances Asian Americans entered the public education pipeline, thus setting the tone for how Asian Americans would eventually be received within the context of higher education. We introduce the idea of students having entered as "raced" individuals and discuss how governments responded to their needs by both extending and restricting their access to public education. Of particular import at the collegiate level is the rise of student activism in the 1960s and 1970s efforts toward the development of ethnic studies programs and providing increased student services for underprivileged youth. In addition to providing a general overview of the aims and opportunities of a public education in the United States and higher education (Rudolph, 1962; Thelin, 2011), we review the role of colleges and universities in serving Asian American students' needs, if at all (Austin, 2007; Daniels, 2003; Douglass, 2007; O'Brien, 1949; Okihiro, 1999; Posadas, 2013; Posadas & Guyotte, 1990, 1992; Synnott, 2010; Tamura, 2001).

The third chapter, *Affirmative Action and Asian American Admissions*, examines the admissions controversies of the 1980s and 1990s in selective colleges and universities. The positioning of Asian American students as having reached the pinnacle of academic success, without the aid of affirmative action policies, leveled a discursive battle over admissions policies mirroring early 20th century admission restrictions against Jewish students (Gorelick, 1981; Karabel, 2005; Levine, 1986; Synnott, 2010). Breaking away from the comparisons with Jewish students, we argue that the ways in which Asian American college attendees in this time period have been discursively framed is based on the extension of the "yellow peril" stereotype (Lee, 2008; Nakanishi, 1989; Takagi, 1998). Coupled with the growing sense of peril was the fear of Asian American overrepresentation on college campuses.

The controversy over admissions cannot be divorced from the larger debates surrounding affirmative action and who can benefit from such policies. The place where Asian Americans became "nonminority" minorities and now "victims" of affirmative action (Lee, 2008) gained momentum from court cases questioning the legality of race in admissions decisions (*Regents of the University of California v. Bakke*, 1978). This chapter examines the pivotal court cases that came to define, or convolute, the precarious place of Asian American students on college campuses and the evolution of campus policies regarding affirmative action. In that vein, we point to various contradictions and ironies in how Asian American students continue to be perceived as being overrepresented.

Largely forgotten in the larger debates over admissions and controversies of affirmative action are how Asian American students themselves actually experience college. In the fourth chapter, *Influential Factors in the Asian American and Pacific Islander College Student Experience*, we highlight emergent research that investigates the range, diversity, and complexity of Asian American students' experiences in higher education (Abelmann, 2009; Garrod & Kilkenny, 2007) including the often-ignored sector of community colleges (Chang, 2005; Chang & Kiang, 2009; Horn & Ethington, 2002; Lew, Chang, & Wang, 2005; Orsuwan, 2011; Wang, Chang, & Lew, 2009). Their experiences reveal the strengths and limitations of structural elements on campuses that work to promote as well as impede students' overall development. Thus, this chapter aims to help inform pedagogy, curriculum, and student services that take into account a holistic evaluation of the Asian American collegiate experience both in and out of the classroom.

Furthermore, this chapter also focuses on the emergence of the Asian American and Native American Pacific Islander–Serving Institutions (AANAPISIs) as a new way of serving the diverse educational needs of these emerging student populations.

In the final chapter, *Conclusions and Recommendations*, we provide a summary of the major points and places where college personnel can begin to develop disaggregated data for Asian American students. Accuracy in data collection can reveal places for developing more culturally relevant student services as well as discontinuing policies that homogenize the experiences of all Asian American students so that they can be considered under programs targeting "underrepresented minorities." We emphasize recommendations and implications for research, policy, and practice.

Defining "Asian American"

For the purposes of this monograph, Asian American and Asian American Pacific Islander (AAPI) are used interchangeably. There remains continued debate over the precise definition of who constitutes an "Asian American." In recent history, the political efforts to mobilize and create a pan-Asian American identity worked favorably toward progressive measures in overcoming discriminatory policies (Espiritu, 1993). However, there have been increasing concerns that a monolithic identity does not capture the particularities of specific ethnic groups' history and subjugation under imperial and colonial powers (Diaz, 2010). The assumption that an Asian American identity is predicated on East Asian origins, as has been typically characterized in recent past, is severely limited. Because of the imprecision of the term, we go beyond the 2010 U.S. Census definition of "Asian" which the federal government defines as a person having origins in any of the original peoples of the Far East, Southeast Asia, or the Indian subcontinent, including, for example, Cambodia, China, India, Japan, Korea, Malaysia, Pakistan, the Philippine Islands, Thailand, and Vietnam (U.S. Census Bureau, 2010). We also include Native Hawaiian and Pacific Islanders (NHPI) in this study as scholarships in Asian American studies have historically included a broader conception of Asian America, all the while being mindful of each ethnic group's particularities with regard to (im)migration, displacement, colonialism, and settlement. Furthermore, the relatively recent establishment of AANAPISIs and the White House Initiative on Asian Americans and Pacific Islanders programs further fosters a sense of pan-Asian American identity that not only recognizes difference within this population but also embraces similarities among the overall immigrant experience. The census has a separate category for NHPI's and defines them as persons having origins in any of the original peoples of Hawaii, Guam, Samoa, or other Pacific Islands (U.S. Census Bureau, 2010). While the NHPI's unique positions are worth investigating in their own right, especially in consideration of their experiences paralleling indigenous populations (Diaz, 2010), we approach the Asian American Pacific Islander (AAPI) category to capture the breadth of students' experiences on college campuses.

We also maintain that to come to a clear definition of who constitutes an "Asian American" remains imprecise as the identification markers have been historically and politically contingent, it is a group still in the making, and also dependent on how the means of identification and definition fluctuates.

An example of the range of Asian American ethnic identities as indicated by several sources, again not exhaustive, is further delineated below:

- *Central Asians*: Afghani, Armenian, Azerbaijani, Georgians, Kazakh, Kyrgyz, Mongolian, Tajik, Turkmen, and Uzbek.
- *East Asians*: Chinese, Japanese, Korean, Okinawan, Taiwanese, and Tibetan.
- *Native Hawaiians and Pacific Islanders* (in the U.S. Jurisdictions and Territories): Carolinian, Chamorro, Chuukese, Fijian, Guamanian, Hawaiian, Kosraean, Marshallesse, Native Hawaiian, Niuean, Palauan, Pohnpeian, Samoan, Tokelauan, Tongan, and Yapese.
- *Southeast Asians*: Bruneian, Burmese, Cambodian, Filipino, Hmong, Indonesian, Laotian, Malaysian, Mien, Papua New Guinean, Singaporean, Timorese, Thai, and Vietnamese.
- *South Asians*: Bangladeshi, Bhutanese, Indian, Maldivians, Nepali, Pakistani, and Sri Lankan.
- *West Asians*: This is a contested term, most people from the region do not self-identify as such. West Asia is typically referred to as the Middle East, and geographically includes the countries of Bahrain, Iran, Iraq, Israel, Jordan, Kuwait, Lebanon, Oman, Palestine, Qatar, Saudi Arabia, Syria, Turkey (straddles Europe and Asia), United Arab Emirates, and Yemen (APIIDV, 2010).

It is outside the bounds of this monograph to examine each ethnic group and we do not purport to be authorities in that regard. What further complicates Asian American identities is the increasing multiracial Asian populations in the United States and the implications for policies and practices at all educational levels (Andrews & Chun, 2007; Espiritu, 2001; Khanna, 2004; Literte, 2010; Root, 1992, 1997; Smith, 2010; Zhang, 2013). We also challenge the inclusion of certain groups within specific AAPI categories listed above, but despite our current understandings, what we are attempting to reveal is how the heterogeneity of group identities become masked by the monolithic perceptions of who Asian Americans are. It is the problematics of perception to reality that we seek to expose.

Research Literature on Race and Asian America

In the past three decades, research on race as it relates to Asian Americans, within the multiracial fabric of U.S. society, has proliferated. What we offer in this section are samples of scholarship that have expanded how we have come to configure Asian Americans not only in the national discourse on race relations but also in its connections to education research.

Race as a Social Construct

Much of the current theoretical understanding of race is attributed to the groundbreaking work of sociologists Omi and Winant (1994). They challenged previous understandings of race and racial categories as fixed and static to one where the process of racial formation was fluid, highly dependent on the gravitational pull of the social and political milieu. The historical contingency of race and racial identity maintains, however, that racism was and is indeed a lived reality, as explicit racial codes barred racial minorities from full civic participation. Structures of oppression sustained themselves in the ways that they did because those in power could define, in those historical moments, and govern those groups to exclude from the larger polity (Omi & Winant, 1994). This idea of the fluidity and power of race has been further explored through an exploration of "whiteness." Proving that racial identity does not only concern people of color, an analysis of the category of White itself is rooted in these processes of race as a social construct. Immigrant groups such as the Irish and Italian, who were much disdained and considered of racially inferior stock, were eventually accepted as "White" and granted all the privileges pertaining to whiteness, such as the ability to lay claim to business interests and political power. The assimilation of these groups under the White category would thus help those in power uphold status quo (Ignatiev, 2008; Roediger, 2005).

The idea of race as a social construct also aids in our understanding of the development of laws specifically aimed against racial minorities, such as anticitizenship and antimiscegenation laws. Laws that sought to restrict citizenship and marriage rights by race in the early 20th century were often contested by Asian Americans based upon supposed rational, literal definitions of the term "race." In 1923, the Supreme Court case of *United States v. Bhagat Singh Thind* denied citizenship to an Indian American U.S. Army veteran because he was not Caucasian. Despite Thind's anthropological evidence that many people from the Indian subcontinent were also of Caucasian ancestry, the court denied Thind's claim to citizenship on the grounds that he was not Caucasian in a common (American) understanding of the term. Furthermore, the 1933 case of *Roldan v. Los Angeles County* challenged California antimiscegenation law on the grounds that the plaintiff, Salvador Roldan, was not barred from interracial marriage because as a Filipino American his race was technically Malay and not "Mongolian," as the law referred to people of Asian descent at the time. Although Roldan's marriage to a Caucasian woman was ruled legal, one month after the case was decided, the California law was amended to also exclude Malay people from marrying Whites (Takaki, 1989). Coupled with the analytic use of race as a social construct are constant streams of references as attached to Asian Americans in U.S. history to the current era: that of the yellow peril and model minority (described in greater detail in the first chapter). These examples of the ways in which race fluctuates based upon historical, geographical, and sociocultural context call for an equally fluid analysis of the way race functions in our everyday lives.

Critical Race Theory and AsianCrit

Building upon the foundational work of Omi and Winant, recent research focusing on the higher educational experiences of Asian Americans has benefited from an emerging analytical framework, Asian Critical Theory (Asian-Crit), rooted in Critical Race Theory (CRT; Chang, 1993). CRT emerged from critical legal studies from leading scholars such as Derrick Bell, Kimberle Crenshaw, Mari Matsuda, Richard Delgado, and Jean Stefancic (Bell, 1993; Crenshaw, Gotanda, & Peller, 1996; Delgado & Stefancic, 2011; Matsuda, Lawrence, Delgado, & Crenshaw, 1993). CRT's influence extended beyond the bounds of legal studies to further extend theoretical developments of race in the social sciences and humanities, including education research (Ladson-Billings & Tate, 1995). Central to their analysis is an ever-present reality that race plays a central role in the ways that laws and subsequent social practices have been enacted over time. Essentially, one cannot examine the legal structures of the nation without a critical read of how laws have worked to disenfranchise already marginalized racial groups. In that vein, CRT places primacy of importance to the notions of race-conscious perspectives (versus color blindness) in understanding how White privilege served to enact normative frames of reality in all formalized structures of society. Understanding how people of color have been victimized through the history of discriminatory laws, including school segregation, and also in everyday social practices through racial microaggressions, requires means of revealing the counternarratives that speak against power (Delgado & Stefancic, 1999, 2011; Matsuda et al., 1993).

Critical Asian Theory (AsianCrit) works specifically to target the experiences of Asian Americans as a racialized and discriminated group in a context that defines race as Black and White. R. S. Chang's (1993, 1999) work in CRT led to the development of an Asian American legal scholarship framework with specificities attached to the Asian American experience such as immigration and citizenship. The recurrent inquisition of "Are you an American?" or "Do you speak English?" work part and parcel to define who can count as an American or not. The wholesale incarceration of over 120,000 Japanese Americans during World War II speaks to how the formulation of foreignness became reified. In that light, Chang and others highlight the unique positioning of Asian Americans in historical and current-day realities to analyze those oppressive forces which work to deny citizenship and immigration rights (Hing, 1993). And while the constant reminder of the outsider racialization (Ancheta, 1997) also affects Latina/o groups in their particularized ways, the specter of the yellow peril and the model minority continues to persist in marginalizing Asian American experiences in ways that are unique to their historical and political context.

In the realm of higher education, emerging CRT scholarship has worked to dispel a number of key misunderstandings about Asian Americans with regard to admissions, affirmative action, race-based scholarship programs, and university practices writ large (Buenavista, 2010; Buenavista, Jayakumar, & Misa-Escalante, 2009; Teranishi, 2010; Teranishi, Behringer, Grey, & Parker, 2009). Identifying Asian American students as a unit of analysis within the constructs of racial formation and framing this group within the lens of

AsianCrit/CRT works toward the development of racially and culturally responsive policies. Critical scholars in education working to dispel the model minority stereotype also find that the perception held by the public is more difficult to overcome within higher education circles, where the stereotype of Asian American excellence and overrepresentation seems to be at its highest because of the social, economic, and cultural implications which are attached to educational attainment at its most elite levels.

Limitations of the Review and Analysis

This monograph identifies key elements and issues affecting Asian American students in higher education and thus does not reflect a comprehensive analysis on the topic. An initial search through various academic database sources yielded thousands of sources related to topics such as the "model minority." The ProQuest Dissertation and Theses database yielded almost 39,000 "hits" when the search phrase "model minority stereotype" was used and over 97,000 results appeared from a search on "Asian Americans in Higher Education." Clearly, these indicate the rapid growth of scholarship, either directly or tangential, on keywords related to Asian Americans. These emerging works are noteworthy to recognize as a number of master's theses and doctoral dissertations will come to have influence in the near future. Given the almost overwhelming amount of scholarship we had to peruse, we were deliberately judicious in our efforts to seek out those publications that adhered to the focus of our study. We take note of recent developments in other related organizations where special issues on and about Asian American students have emerged (e.g., McEwen, Kodama, Alvarez, Lee, & Liang, 2002; Museus, Maramba, & Teranishi, 2013; National Commission on Asian American and Pacific Islander Research in Education [CARE], 2008, 2010, 2011). Taken as a whole, these studies are helping to reshape how we can come to think about the role of higher education institutions in serving diverse populations.

Further studies that capture the qualitative experiences of particular subgroups, especially among the underrepresented and at-risk AAPIs, would provide an enhanced view of the college experience in combination with extant quantitative data already available (Yeh, 2002, 2004). For example, the recent settlement of Karen refugees to Chicago and their transition into community colleges can enhance the growing area of research on APAs in community college settings. Studies that also examine particular gendered experiences among AAPI groups warrant further investigation. A particular stream could focus on AAPI females in STEM fields as, on the one hand, they belong to an "overrepresented" group, but on the other hand, they are also identified as a group needing more representation in STEM fields. Initial findings related to this area have already begun (George-Jackson, 2011). A study that also focuses on multiracial AAPI students on college campuses and how they come to identify themselves in the 21st century would be worthy of investigation (Andrews & Chun, 2007; Literte, 2010). Equally important would be in expanding scholarship that examines the intersectional identities of Asian American students on campuses from the framework of sexual identities and the interplay of culture, acculturation, and religion (Okazaki, 2002). While we cannot extensively explore these and countless other topics, it is our objective to synthesize a breadth of literature which will hopefully lay the foundation for critical lenses of analysis which can guide research on Asian Americans in higher education in a multitude of directions moving forward.

It is upon this foundational context of Asian American experiences throughout the higher education pipeline of students, staff, faculty, and administrators that we now base our research and insight regarding the current trajectory of Asian American students. In the first chapter, we begin by providing an overview of the development of the model minority stereotype and how that ideology managed to remain a strong foothold through the decades.

Historical Overview of the Model Minority Concept

Are Asian Americans Considered Racial Minorities in Higher Education?

While the stereotype of Asian Americans as "model minorities"—naturally gifted, hard-working, and socially passive—is often perceived by Asian Americans and non-Asian Americans alike as a "positive stereotype," many scholars have revealed that Asian American students face double barriers based on the model minority stereotype. They are touted as superachievers, not requiring special programs for recruitment and retention efforts, but at the same time, they face limitations in opportunities based on the assumptions of their overrepresentation, especially in relation to the more underrepresented Asian American ethnic groups (Hune, 2002, 2011; Teranishi, 2010; Teranishi et al., 2009). Touting overachievement yet remaining fearful of overrepresentation points to the precarious position Asian Americans have occupied in society as a whole, and not merely higher education. Thus, the model minority is constantly in dialogue with another established Asian American stereotype—the "yellow peril." Between these two stereotypes, Asian Americans are hypersuccessful academically or they constitute a threat to the normative structure of thinking about race relations. Throughout history, these ideas have undergirded the prevailing notion that Asian Americans exist outside the framework of normalcy. In what legal scholar Angelo Ancheta has termed "outsider racialization" (Ancheta, 1997), the ways in which Asian Americans have been

---

constructed in our social and political history have rested on ensuring their "forever foreigner" status (Tuan, 1999). Despite the concept of race itself as a social construct, the racial formation (Omi & Winant, 1994) of minorities in the United States has resulted in reified structural laws and practices that produced very real and legitimate stratification of life chances and limited access to upward mobility for all people of color, including Asian Americans.

The current minority status of Asian Americans in higher education has certainly come to challenge prevalent understandings of American racial relations since the 1960s and 1970s, when Asian Americans were fully integrated and included in the civil rights and affirmative action discourse. On many college campuses, particularly those elite private and public institutions, the status of Asian American students as minorities (or not) depends on certain organizational interests. On the one hand, Asian Americans may be included in promoting diversity in terms of college enrollment and praised as contributing toward an inclusive environment. On the other hand, however, services typically reserved for minority students, such as affirmative action in admissions, financial aid for underrepresented/underprivileged students, and diversity-related programming efforts in academic and student services, become severely limited or even foreclosed from Asian Americans. For example, the National Science Foundation (NSF) does not consider AAPIs as an "underrepresented" group, thereby excluding them from grants and other financial support (Teranishi, Maramba, & Ta, 2012). A number of higher education institutions, such as the University of Illinois, follow NSF's definition and further lay exclusionary practices for campus-wide fellowships aimed at underrepresented minorities. Some Asian American groups, such as the 80–20 Educational Foundation, and those in the mainstream have held firmly to the belief of Asian American students' overachievement, claiming that affirmative action efforts inhibit the process of meritocracy to come to fruition (further fueling the debate of African American, American Indian, and Latina/o underachievement).

Conversely, proponents for race-conscious measures to include Asian Americans contend that despite significant gains by some, most Asian Americans still remain heavily underrepresented in multiple aspects of the university, including but not limited to non-STEM academic programs, staff, faculty, and civil service workers (e.g., Hune, 2006; Maramba, 2011a; Maramba & Nadal, 2013). Therefore, the question of whether or not Asian Americans are a racial minority within higher education inevitably raises the question of where the boundaries of higher education are drawn, and which characterizations of "majorities" and "minorities" are given primacy over others.

The Various Shades of the Yellow Peril

The idea of Asians constituting an overrepresented minority, and as a potential threat, became popularized with the phrase "yellow peril." During the Gold Rush era of the 19th century, the United States saw a vast migration wave to the West Coast from far and wide, and Chinese immigration was a significant aspect of this population boom. Like many other (predominantly male) sojourners from the United States and abroad, the prospect of finding wealth became the pull factor bringing them to burgeoning cities that were created on their way to the Yukon territories (Chan, 1991).

The popularization of the phrase "yellow peril" is attributed to writer and journalist Jack London in his writings for the Hearst newspapers of the Russo-Japanese war in 1904 (Métraux, 2010). The term itself is believed to have come from German Kaiser Wilhelm II following Japan's defeat of China in 1895 in the first Sino-Japanese War, signaling Japan's rise to military and industrial powers at the time. "Soon, however, it took on a broader more sinister meaning embracing all of Asia. The 'Yellow Peril' highlighted diverse fears including the supposed threat of military invasion from Asia, competition to the white labor force from Asian American workers, the moral degeneracy of Asian people, and the specter of genetic mixing of Anglo-Saxons with Asians" (Métraux, 2010, para. 3). Other historians provide further evidence of how the transnational migration of Asians across the America in the mid-19th century created and reshaped the idea of the yellow peril as a more imminent threat on a global scale (E. Lee, 2007), expanding beyond the boundaries of the United States.

Such fears would work to enforce race-based restrictions against Asian immigration in the United States through the Page Act (1875), Chinese

Exclusion Act (1882), Gentlemen's Agreement (1907), and the Asiatic barred-zone Immigration Act (1917), virtually curtailing any immigration from Asia. Each of these laws was implemented to contest any sort of Asian presence in the social, cultural, economic, and political landscapes of America. Domestically they were also complemented by various laws, which prevented Asian Americans from naturalizing as citizens, owning property, and marrying interracially, among many other *de facto* restrictions. In 1952, the McCarran–Walter Act overturned aspects of the restrictive Immigration Act of 1924 and also provided more limited entry of Asians to immigrate to the United States. More than a decade later, the Immigration and Nationality Act of 1965 overturned all restrictive aspects of the 1924 Immigration Act and allowed for more open immigration to the United States from all over the world, giving preference to family reunification and trained professionals in American industries short on labor. The significance of the act's passage accounts for the majority of Asian American population growth in the country today.

Figure 2 provides the historical growth of Asian American populations in the United States, with projected growth, which reveals the significance of immigration policies post-1960s.

The Asian American and Pacific Islander population is an ever-growing and diverse group, where new ethnic groups continue to arrive under various circumstances. More recent waves of Asian Americans who are immigrating to the United States through family reunification immigration policies may differ from earlier waves of post-1965 immigrants who directly benefited from job placement through company sponsorship of their visas. Without these same benefits, newer Asian immigrants are therefore often subject to underemployment and nontraditional familial living arrangements where extended families (grandparents, adult siblings, nieces, nephews, cousins, etc.) beyond the prototypical nuclear family arrangement cohabit. Furthermore, the arrival of Southeast Asian groups from war-torn countries, such as Vietnam, Cambodia, and Laos from the 1970s through the 1990s, has troubled the popular conception of the overachieving, affluent model minority, which was largely based on stereotypes of East Asian immigrants. Rather than migrating under ideal circumstances, these waves of refugees arrived in the United

FIGURE 2
Asian American and Pacific Islander Population in the Millions in the United States (1860–2050)

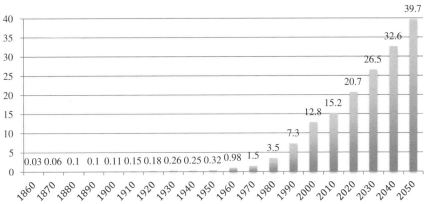

Source: U.S. Census Bureau, Population Division. (2011). From "The Relevance of Asian American and Pacific Islanders in the College Completion Agenda" (p. 4). *The National Commission on Asian American and Pacific Islanders Research in Education.* Adapted with permission.

States without the same resources as other Asian American immigrants who had higher education degrees, training for professional careers, and a greater degree of freedom to choose their place of settlement. Thus, it is significant to note that because Southeast Asians did not easily fit within the frames of public reference of being the successful Asian, some have come to be "ideologically blackened" (Ong, 2003). This term signifies those Asians, southeast in particular, who become categorized as criminals and cultural delinquents who defy the common conception of the model minority. Thus, Southeast Asians are racialized in a manner that upholds status quo in two ways: (a) as immigrant refugees from Asia, they are considered part of the yellow peril that is supposedly overpopulating the country and (b) taking opportunities away from deserving Americans. Furthermore, their ideological blackening separates them from the predominantly East Asian model minority, labeling them as outliers who are simply not treated as part of the discourse of Asian America, but rather a marginalized "Other" that does not fit into any preconceived notion of racial mores.

Asian Americans in Higher Education

The Modern "Model Minority" Emerges

The passage of the 1965 Immigration Act, which facilitated an influx of Asian immigration, and the simultaneous time period of sweeping civil rights legislation converged to create an interesting historical moment. While one event did not directly influence the other, the processes of change that occurred during that time gave way for the modern model minority stereotype to emerge. With African Americans at the forefront in fomenting structural changes for equality and equity under the law, the clamor that it raised, in the minds of many, necessitated a counter response. With the passage of the Civil Rights Act of 1964 and the Immigration and Nationality Act of 1965, the United States had seemingly ended all forms of institutionalized discrimination. In search of a means to purport the political successes of these new legislations on both a domestic and an international level, Asian Americans were chosen as the poster children of a new equitable American ideal, which was presumably attained via a meritocratic and equal-footed quest.

It should be noted, however, that how Asians have been politically and racially positioned was nothing new. Scholars have noted how popular culture's lauding of Chinese immigrants' predilection for hard work and obedience was used in comparison to freed slaves during Reconstruction and Irish immigrants in the North (Wu, 2003). Ironically, however, while the Chinese were noted for their work ethic, they (Asians writ large) were still seen as unfit for citizenship in the debates that led up to the ratification of the 14th Amendment supposedly extending citizenship rights to African Americans and securing equal protection under the law (Anderson, 2007). The now deliberate reemergence of Asian Americans as the model minority in the 1960s became popularized through two early publications. One of the most often-cited references comes from University of California, Berkeley, sociologist, William Petersen's (1966) *New York Times Magazine* article, "Success Story, Japanese-American Style." The article begins by asking which minority group in the United States faced some of its worst atrocities, thus drawing comparisons between the types of injustices which have occurred and inevitably assigning ordinal effects which favored some forms of discrimination and prejudice over others:

Asked which of the country's ethnic minorities has been subjected to the most discrimination and the worse injustices, very few persons would even think of answering: "The Japanese Americans." Yet, if the question refers to persons alive today, that may well be the correct reply. Like the Negroes, the Japanese have been the object of color prejudice. Like the Jews, they have been feared and hated as hyperefficient competitors. And, more than any other group, they have been seen as agents of an overseas enemy. . . Generally this kind of treatment as we all know these days, creates what might be termed "problem minorities." (Petersen, 1966, pp. 20–21)

Petersen further notes that to reshape the structural flaws that enacted discrimination would be a futile attempt, as it could not be overturned, even with the newly enacted civil rights laws. The jab against African Americans in their continuous quest for civic freedom was seen as a mockery. Instead, Petersen sought to portray how Japanese Americans found a way to overcome the immediate past discrimination and to even flourish in American culture. He lists a bevy of oppressive government measures under which Japanese Americans suffered in the 20th century (antimiscegenation laws, anticitizenship and anti-immigration laws, and wartime internment) to argue against civil rights expansion for African Americans. The significant features of this article pointed to the Japanese Americans' cultural resistance toward seeking governmental support (i.e., welfare) and instead relying on one's individual efforts (an extension of the Protestant work ethic) toward social mobility. The tone of Petersen's article also suggests that African Americans were clamoring all for naught, as the vestiges of slavery were too entrenched to overturn discrimination against them. It also signified the popularity of mainstream sentiment that gained increased attention from a 1965 report authored by then-Assistant Secretary of Labor Daniel Patrick Moynihan, entitled *The Negro Family: The Case for National Action*. Otherwise known as the Moynihan Report, it laid claims to the features of the culture of poverty stemming from the lack of a nuclear family structure (the traditional family structure for which Asian Americans were lauded). The rise of single-mother households and an absent father figure were the cultural byproducts of the system of enslavement that continued to plague the Black family, as Moynihan would assert. The ways in which the report portrayed how Black culture reinforced its own cycle of poverty through ignorance and complacency could not be overturned through governmental legislation.

This depiction of Asian Americans worked in contradistinction to the struggle for equal rights that had been spearheaded by African Americans for more than a century, demanding full recognition and rights under the law, as promised in the 14th Amendment of the U.S. Constitution. Pointing to individual or cultural explanations for social (im)mobility, rather than to systems of entrenched structural discrimination, the influence and legacy of the Moynihan Report still exists to explain one group's achievement (i.e., Asian Americans) and another group's failure (African Americans and Latinos, in aggregate).

Adding increased support to the modern model minority stereotype came through another article by the *U.S. News & World Report* (1966), "Success Story of One Minority Group in U.S." The authors, claiming to have scoured Chinatowns across the country, remarked at the high levels of discipline, hard work, and promotion of traditional family values. Indeed, criminal activities were low and all the youth were actively engaged in their studies, obeying their fathers and mothers to maintain traditional Chinese culture while promoting American values of hard work and thrift. As the opening of the article makes clear:

> *At a time when Americans are awash in worry over the plight of racial minorities—One such minority, the nation's 300,000 Chinese-Americans, is winning wealth and respect by dint of its own hard work. In any Chinatown from San Francisco to New York, you discover youngsters at grips with their studies. Crime and delinquency are found to be rather minor in scope. Still being taught in Chinatown is the old idea that people should depend on their own efforts—not a welfare check—in order to reach American's "promised land." (U.S. News & World Report, 1966, p. 6).*

The indirect reference to African Americans in this article no longer placed Asian Americans in the same struggle with all racial minorities, but rather, as a new type of "model" minority to which all other minorities should aspire, arguably even with which to compete. The obvious question became, "They made it without government support, why can't you?" However, no considerations were given to the relative disparities in resource allocation, reparations, immigration status, and other social, cultural, economic, and political rights which were selectively distributed among people of color and continued to perpetuate stratified life chances and curtail social mobility for a majority of people of color long after institutionalized discrimination was written out of public policy.

This form of racial triangulation of Asian Americans (Kim, 1999) would set the stage for continuous false comparisons between and among minorities and the mainstream, especially in the post–Civil Rights era. In delineating the concept of racial triangulation, political scientist Claire Jean Kim (1999) demonstrates that the end result is to place Whites at the top of the hierarchy of the racial order by positioning Asian Americans below them as "honorary Whites" and above African Americans (and Latinos). This form of "relative valorization," placing Asian Americans betwixt the Black/White binary, maintains the dominance of Whites over both groups. Furthermore, Kim (1999) emphasizes that while Asian Americans are situated above African Americans in the racial hierarchy, the processes of "civic ostracism" work to construct and subordinate Asian Americans as "immutably foreign and unassimilable with Whites on cultural and/or racial grounds in order to ostracize them from the body politic and civic membership" (p. 107).

The historical persistence of racial triangulation as it relates to Asian Americans, being racially positioned above African Americans yet not ever achieving full civic status, is long and has been clearly documented (Kurashige, 2007; Wu, 2003). The 1990 Flatbush Boycott in Brooklyn, NY, and the Los Angeles Riots in 1992 speak to some of the more recent problematic effects of interracial violence (especially between African Americans and Koreans) stemming from Asian Americans' precarious racial positioning in recent decades (Kim, 2003). As these struggles over equal opportunities continued throughout the second half of the 20th century, the realm of public education naturally became yet another arena of debate regarding the allocation of public resources and the pursuit of equitable rights.

The Model Minority Goes to School

It is within this political and social backdrop, praising Asian Americans' rugged individual collectivist cultural tendencies while denigrating African Americans' dependence on social welfare programs, that the noticeable attention on Asian Americans moved into education discourse. With the model minority emphasizing concepts of socioeconomic mobility, obedience and passivity, and concentration in high-paying, scientific jobs, the implications of this stereotype inevitably trickled down into the education system, particularly higher education. Claims of Asian American exceptionalism in academics as the new discourse of the immigrant success story worked its way into the public schools. The 1980s witnessed the rise of the Asian American "whiz kid" (Brand, 1987), from Westinghouse prizewinners to the National Spelling Bee champions. The presence of Asian Americans as academically successful was ubiquitous. Cultural and even biological explanations were given to provide "evidence" for the students' academic prowess (Ng et al., 2007) in much the same way that these pseudosciences were used to explain Asians' cultural deficiencies and inability to assimilate less than a century prior. Subsequent research on students and schools set out to seek why Asian American students were so successful—already operating under the assumption that this phenomenon was true rather than asking if those constructs were true in the first place. Even a cursory glance at educational research on the achievement gap points to the assumed success of Asian American students (Peng & Wright, 1994). The latest report by the Pew Research Center (2012) further perpetuates the idea of the success of AAPI's in education and household income earnings. As the report summarily claims, Asian Americans place more value than other Americans do on marriage, parenthood, hard work, and career success (Pew Research Center, 2012). Such statements fundamentally assume simultaneously that hard work and commitment to education by Asian Americans are inherent traits independent of any environmental influences and that the perceived lack of these characteristics among other racial minority groups is a rational and conscious choice to be complacent with one's position in an underclass of society. This dichotomy which places Asian Americans at a permanent advantage and other people of color at a permanent disadvantage treats those who do not fit the mold on either end of the spectrum as outliers whose experiences are anomalies, rather than important trends which should be analyzed in order to effectively address students' needs and bolster their capabilities. In other words, it reduces educational experiences to quantifiable trends rather than addressing the qualitative nature of educational outcomes that goes beyond standardized test scores and grade point averages.

Thus, in discussing the true impact of education and the attainment of specific educational outcomes by Asian American students, it is important to note the wide range of AAPI students' experiences along the P–20 pipeline as many, even those who seemingly do well academically, report higher levels of depression, stress, and suicidal tendencies (Cheng et al., 2010). Particularly salient are the experiences of Filipinos in this context. Approximately 3.2 million Filipinos reside in the United States, the second largest ethnic group behind Chinese (3.7 million). Nearly 36.7% of Filipino adults have college degrees, which tend to be higher than other Asian ethnic subgroups, but there exists challenges U.S. Filipino youth face in entering postsecondary institutions. Filipino immigrant and second-generation youth exhibit high secondary "push out" rates, suffer from depression and other mental health issues, demonstrate lower levels of participation and retention in higher education, face challenges in the college environment, and attend less selective colleges if they pursue postsecondary education (Buenavista, 2010; Choi, 2008; Maramba, 2008a, 2008b; Maramba & Bonus, 2013; Nadal, Pituc, Johnston, & Esparrago, 2010). Further complicating their experiences are the assumptions of monolithically identifying them as successful Asian Americans. In contrast to other Asian Americans, Filipinos are the only Asian Americans whose homeland was colonized by the United States, thus establishing a tenuous relationship between Filipinos and the U.S. government. Many Filipino American students, despite having the advantages and privileges conducive to high achievement in education, such as middle class socioeconomic status and English predominantly spoken in the household, are often racialized and negatively treated as non-Asians due to their typically darker phenotype, and thus denied the appropriate counseling and guidance by educational professionals (Teranishi, 2010). Furthermore, they are often not targeted or eligible for institution-sponsored postsecondary access and retention programs, and often cannot receive similar benefits from their parents, who, despite being college educated, mostly received their degrees in the Philippines and thus are relatively unaware of the nuanced aspects of the American higher education experience. But in the context of color-blind educational discourse, their issues have been rendered largely invisible (Buenavista, 2010).

The current relationship between Filipino Americans and higher education is only one example of the manifestation of stressors that relate, either implicitly or explicitly, from the structural beliefs of AAPI as the model minority. These trends have begun to increase awareness within college counseling and psychological literature, especially in relation to mental health (Hyun, Quinn, Madon, & Lustig, 2006; Ly, 2008) and relationships to immigrant or refugee family status (Meekyung, 2005). As a predominantly immigrant community, issues of acculturation and intergenerational conflict constitute significant dissonance within the lives of all Asian Americans. Whether in service to school age youth or to adults within the AAPI communities, mental health awareness and education have received growing priority among mental health practitioners for many decades (Sue & McKinney, 1975; Sue, Yan Cheng, Saad, & Chu, 2012; Uba, 2003). Current psychological research concludes that Asian Americans are the racial group least likely to pursue mental health counseling due to cultural values of stigma and self-reliance. Therefore, outreach to these communities regarding mental health must be proactive in order to effectively address the needs of Asian Americans (Suzuki, 2002). It is not enough to merely establish resources that are for anyone and everyone to help. Mental health professionals and educational administrators must collaborate in order to actively reach out to communities who may not be immediately aware of the effects of counseling or even the institutions within the school system or the community at large responsible for delegating such services to students.

Without a doubt, Asian American students in our K–12 systems have high variability of performance at all levels and structures of schooling and their needs and capabilities must be effectively addressed through pedagogy, curriculum, and institutional support of teachers, students, and parents (Pang, Han, & Pang, 2011). Immigration status, parents' educational levels, gender, English language fluency, native language fluency, residential patterns, and socioeconomic status are just a few examples of factors that shape students' lives and school performance (Kao, 1995; Kao & Thompson, 2003). Where research indicates that Asian Americans are high achieving, it typically tends to occur more frequently among East Asian and South Asian Americans, although recent scholarship also troubles notions of achievement based on class and religion among these groups (Asher, 2008; Joshi, 2006; Lew, 2006a, 2006b). However, rather than being skewed toward the higher end of the spectrum as the model minority myth leads many to believe, AAPI educational attainment typically remains bimodal, clustering in two different groups, with large numbers of high performers at one end and large numbers of relatively low performers at the other (Aoki & Takeda, 2008; Chew-Ogi & Ogi, 2002). In gauging educational attainment by those AAPI subethnic groups, Figure 3 makes visually clear the bimodal educational attainment levels of those among Asian Indian, Chinese, Pakistani, and Korean in contrast to Samoan, Tongan, Native Hawaiian, Guamanian, Hmong, Laotian, and Cambodian groups.

Southeast Asian and Pacific Islander students face, on average, more dissonant experiences within the school structure. Some of the seminal research on Southeast Asian Americans indicates high degrees of academic struggles and a foreclosing of higher education opportunities stemming from a host of personal and academic issues that include complications of gender, class, and language (CARE, 2011; Maramba, 2011b; Museus, 2009; Ngo, 2006; Ngo & Lee, 2007). And where they do not fit within that model of success, they are castigated as juvenile delinquents—criminalized and racialized in very similar ways to African American students who may "act up" as they come "up against whiteness" (Lee, 2005). In what Aihwa Ong considers the process of being "ideologically blackened" (Ong, 2003), many Asian American youth exist in the "Black/White" binary where not being like the prototypical high-performing Asian (which is designated as an "honorary White" category)

FIGURE 3

Educational Attainment for Asian American and Pacific Islander College Attendees, by Ethnic Sub-Group (Age 25 or Older, 2006–2008)

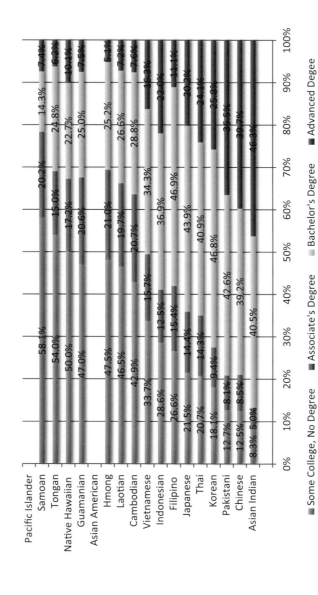

Some College, No Degree   Associate's Degree   Bachelor's Degree   Advanced Degree

Note: Data reported for individuals with at least some college.

Source: American Community Survey, 3-Year Public Use Microdata Sample (PUMS). (2011). From "The Relevance of Asian American and Pacific Islanders in the College Completion Agenda" (p. 11). *The National Commission on Asian American and Pacific Islanders Research in Education.* Adapted with permission.

renders them to the "underachieving" category that plagues students such as African American and Latino males.

What we have noted here in terms of Asian American students in K–12 barely skims the surface, but we wanted to reveal the layers of complexity also involved in what being an Asian American student means in our school systems. Scholars who examine AAPI issues at the K–12 level have done much to expand understandings of such complex dynamics from multiple viewpoints. These works point to how school systems, operating under the assumption of innate and unwavering Asian American success, fail to understand students as individuals with their own particular needs and support systems (Pang & Cheng, 1998). Other realities that affect AAPI students in our schools concern incidents of bullying, racialized hate crimes, and growing anti-Asian incidents on K–12 and higher education arenas, particularly where South Asians are seen as "terrorists" (Sikh Coalition, Asian American Legal Defense and Education Fund [AALDEF], and the New York Civil Liberties Union [NYCLU], 2010). While all of these may not come as a direct result of the model minority myth, the literature would contend that it contributes, among others, to increased hostile feelings between students (both within and between racial/ethnic groups) and creates unnecessary comparisons on the part of school officials between Asians and all other groups. As Stacey Lee (1996) notes, the image of the model minority is a hegemonic device that denies difference within Asian American communities, and more importantly, "maintains the dominance of whites in the racial hierarchy by diverting attention away from racial inequality and by setting standards for how minorities should behave" (p. 6). The means of internalization of the model minority myth in and out of groups and the perceptions attached to it become reified and continue to support the process of racial triangulation.

On a larger scale affecting K–12 education, recent court cases that have effectively scaled back efforts to promote diversity (*Parents Involved in Community Schools v. Seattle School District*, 2007) indicate a long-standing effect post-1954 *Brown v. Board of Education* whereby our nation's public schools have become highly resegregated. Orfield and Lee's (2007) study provides a compilation of data that indicate the nation's racial minority students attend schools that are the most segregated. In other words, students attend schools with those who most match their racial and ethnic background. Orfield and Lee contend, however, that Asian students (they do not use the term "Asian American" in their study) attend the most integrated schools in that less than a fourth of fellow students are Asian and typically attend schools that are 48% White, compared to 32% for Latinos. On average, Asian (Americans) attend schools that are 24% Asian (Orfield & Lee, 2007). This schooling pattern is a result of residential (re)settlement patterns which have historically been the product of the discriminatory market actions of "White flight" which have both explicitly and implicitly controlled who lives where (Bonilla-Silva, 2009). And while Orfield has investigated the effects of segregation in the K–12 realm post-Brown, there is a limitation of understanding how school resegregation influences the ways in which AAPI students experience schooling.

Considering that AAPIs attend schools within AAPI prevalent communities, there exists the potential of schools to underserve the needs of students within particular linguistic, educational, and economic contexts. These AAPI students are most at-risk of experiencing cultural and linguistic isolation in the public schools and are the least likely of all students to find any significant representation of their own ethnicity or hear their native language being spoken by peers and teachers (NEA, 2008). Students who have immigrated from Southeast Asian countries, especially since the post-Vietnam era, are most likely to experience linguistic isolation, a shortage of cultural or community resources, and instruction from educators who are not culturally competent (NEA, 2008). In particular, Vietnamese, Cambodian, and Hmong students comprise the underrepresented AAPI populations who defy the model minority stereotype. More often they come from households with parents who hold lower levels of educational degrees and lower levels of income resulting in increased poverty (CARE, 2011). Segregated environments continue to hamper potential relationships across racial and class divides and in considering the role of peer networks for adolescent youth, diversity can also create positive social outcomes for students of all races and ethnicities, not just underrepresented Asian Americans (Goza & Ryabov, 2009).

This needed digression into aspects of K–12 education is important as it becomes the foundation upon which we can understand not only *who* goes

FIGURE 4
Proportion of AAPI Adults Without a High School Diploma Equivalent by Ethnicity (2000)

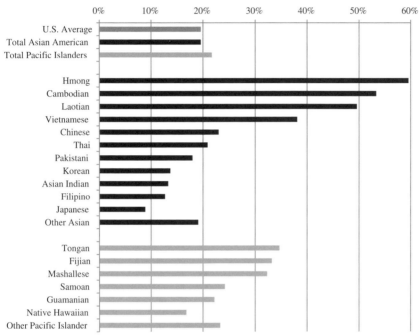

Note: Data reported for adults, ages 25 or over.
Source: Teranishi, R. T. (2010). "Analysis of data from the U.S. Census Bureau (2000), Summary File 4." *Asians in the Ivory Tower* (p. 110). New York, NY: Teachers College Press. Adapted with permission.

to college but also how, why, and where (e.g., two-year or four-year, public or private, highly selective or not, etc.). As Figure 4 demonstrates, when disaggregated by Asian ethnic categories of those group members who do not hold a high school diploma, Southeast Asian and Pacific Islander adults are 2–3 times more likely to not have attained a diploma. Nearly 60% of Hmong Americans do not have a high school diploma, followed by Cambodian (53%), Laotian (48%), Vietnamese (38%), Tongan (35%), Fijian (33%), Marshallese (32%), and Samoan (24%). These are well above the U.S. national average hovering at 20%. Clearly, how Southeast Asian and Pacific Islander groups experience their adjustment to mainstream society and the cultural mismatch that can occur in schools contributes to the challenges they face and that lay ahead. When aggregated for the whole the total Asian American (exclusive of Pacific Islanders) population without a high school diploma mirrors the national average. This statistic in and of itself may challenge the model minority myth of achievement. Nonetheless, to gauge Asian American educational levels in the aggregate hides more important factors of the major differences among various ethnic groups. Such factors may be environmental which go beyond monolithic categorizations of some mythical predilection toward excellence.

In the next chapter, we expand our discussions regarding the model minority myth to address additional facets of the myth that characterize Asian Americans as passive and apolitical. By covering the general history of Asian American student presence on college campuses in the 20th century, we aim to establish how the very presence of Asian Americans in higher education is largely attributed to the development of the Civil Rights Movement and subsequent Asian American participation in multiracial student coalitions calling for increased diversity and representation at all levels of higher education.

Asian Americans and the Educational Pipeline: Tenuous Citizenship

THROUGHOUT EVERY ASPECT OF THE educational pipeline from the student body through the highest levels of administration, a comprehensive history of education as it pertains to Asian American groups is sorely lacking (Tamura, 2001, 2003). Where educational historiography exists, it is typically embedded within the histories of particular ethnic groups (Low, 1982; Tamura, 1993) or is connected to particular schooling experiences during World War II and beyond, with a primary focus on second-generation Japanese Americans, or Nisei (Pak, 2001). Some of the major historical works on education center on the theme of the legal and social barriers to educational opportunities and access in light of school segregation policies (Wollenberg, 1978). To be sure, the scarce literature on Asian American student experiences in higher education certainly calls for more research to be conducted in this area. This chapter highlights some of the movements within higher education in the late 19th and 20th centuries that provided increased access for both Asian international and Asian American students. While there are distinct experiences and histories between these two groups of students that resulted in segmented access to higher education, particularly pre-1965, it is important to point out how access to higher education for Asian American students, which occurred much later in the 20th century, was a result of the embodiment of a pan-ethnic Asian American identity that united various ethnic groups under common interests that were believed to be mutually beneficial for not just all Asian Americans, but for all students from underrepresented communities.

The first Asian college student on record in the United States was Yung Wing, a graduate of Yale College in 1854 (Worthy, 1965). He arrived in the United States as a teenager under the sponsorship of Samuel Robbins Brown, a Yale graduate and missionary, who opened the first Protestant school in China where he taught Wing. Influenced by his western education and possessing a deep desire to assist in reforms in China, Wing later convinced the Chinese government to support an establishment of the Chinese Education Mission (CEM) that officially began in 1872. It was in some ways a radical break from tradition as the early group of Chinese students went overseas to study abroad. Between 1872 and 1875, 120 young men arrived in the New England area to acquire a Western education and vocational training to ultimately assist in the reform efforts in China (Chinese Educational Mission, n.d.). The complications of adjusting to life in a new country, administrative tensions between Yung Wing and members of the Chinese government over the kind of education the students should attain, as well as the unintended results of social and personal acculturation processes among the youth ultimately led to the disbanding of the program in 1881.

While there are more intricate pieces of this history that have been documented, among them being Wing's autobiography (Wing, 1909), a glimpse into the secondary sources reveals an individual who straddled loyalties between China and the United States; his desire was to embrace both. Clearly he wished to become an American citizen. He eventually attained naturalized citizenship status in 1852, married a White woman, produced two offspring, and settled in New Haven. But once the U.S. government began to question his business and governmental affairs in China, the air of suspicion ultimately resulted in revoking his U.S. citizenship (Worthy, 1965). Toward the end of his life, he lived in obscurity and poverty but his influence is still deeply felt. In fact, the Yung Wing School P.S. 124 (2008) in New York's Chinatown is named after him for his pioneering efforts in higher education.

In the early 20th century, following the presence of Chinese students on college campuses, the Filipino Pensionado program was established to provide college education to the sons of Filipino elites who succumbed to U.S. rule in the aftermath of the Spanish–American War. Historians Barbara Posadas and Roland Guyotte, who have written extensively on this topic, note that in 1903 the first of the pensionados, government-sponsored scholarship students, were chosen from each Philippine province to receive an education in the United States. The students first spent a year in high school (1903–1904) together to get acclimated to American language and culture and were then dispersed to colleges and universities along the East Coast and the Midwest (Posadas & Guyotte, 1990). Even in more remote locales such as DeKalb, Illinois, six pensionado pioneers enrolled at the State Normal School in DeKalb (now Northern Illinois University). In the state of Illinois alone, a total of 42 (including the DeKalb six) pensionados would attend the University of Chicago, Lewis Institute (Chicago), Armour Institute (Chicago), the University of Illinois, the State Normal Schools at Normal and Macomb, and Dixon Business College outside of Chicago (Posadas, 2013). The development of a Filipino American community in Chicago grew as a result of these pensionados. In the first decade of the 20th century, nearly one quarter of the nation's pensionados enrolled in U.S. institutions of higher education studied in Illinois (Posadas, 2013). Though their presence in urban centers such as Chicago and the formation of an ethnic community cemented their place in society, the perception of Filipinos as foreigners remained (Posadas & Guyotte, 1990, 1992). Filipino student groups at the University of Illinois, for example, were organized as an international student group, even though they were technically considered U.S. citizens (Andal, 2002).

The Midwest as a site for early Asian American community formation via university students could be considered anathema to the dominant narrative of labor migration to the West Coast. However, the Pensionado program and the establishment of an "Open Door" policy toward Chinese graduate students at the University of Illinois at Urbana-Champaign would prove to be significant on multiple fronts, the least of which would be in recognizing the long history of Asian presence in America's heartland. Whereas the traditional scholarship on Asian American history has rested on the immigration of labor workers, very few have concentrated on the migration of intellectuals (Espiritu, 2005; Posadas, 2013; Yu, 2001). In investigating Illinois as an example of early Asian college and graduate students, we witness the particularities of their cases. The exempt class of Chinese immigrant students, who could enter the United States during the Chinese exclusion era, would find the University of Illinois a more hospitable locale stemming from the liberal admissions policies enacted by then University President Edmund J. James and his predecessors (Huang, 2001). From 1910 to 1954 (and until the 1960s) the University of Illinois graduated the highest numbers of doctorate awardees in the country and averaged almost 18% of total enrollment of Chinese students in the United States (Huang, 2001). The early Chinese intellectuals on campus would influence the development of Chinese higher education institutions, politics and businesses upon their graduation and return to China, effectively establishing globalizing networks of transnational relations. As Huang (2001) notes, "In short, the formation of a local Chinese student community involved many factors in international diplomacy, trade, the development of American transnational corporation in Asia and intellectual aspiration of American and Chinese educators; American business ventures in China; and networks of family, classmates, friends, relatives, teachers, and institutions such as schools and universities and governments" (p. 303).

The presence of Asian students on college campuses, even in small Midwestern towns, was a clear indication of the intricate web of global relationships sparked by the pursuit of higher education. However, to solely focus on these students overshadows the complexities of the K–12 educational pipeline that Asian American students often had to contest and navigate before even getting to the collegiate level. The struggles that occurred within the K–12 realm in the first part of the 20th century would establish a new attitude toward public education as America continued to diversify. Education very quickly became a commodity that was vehemently sought after by those wrongfully excluded from it, and just as passionately protected by those with exclusive access to it.

Asian American Access to the Educational Pipeline

A noteworthy aspect of early Asian students in higher education is that they came from other places, that is, there is little record of Asian Americans attending colleges and universities in the late 19th and early 20th centuries.

Certainly, immigration restrictions on Asian entry into the United States since the late 1880s would curtail not only entry but also subsequent creation of new generations of offspring who might have had a small chance at going to college. But another connection to examine here is how school segregation laws in the public schools foreclosed any opportunity for admission and attendance in higher education. This hostile climate toward Asian Americans in public schools and the effects that institutionalized segregation had on shutting off Asian American students from the educational pipeline altogether are indicative of the highly flammable sociopolitical aspects of education which go far beyond the individual acts of achievement within the classroom environment.

Tape v. Hurley (1885)

One of the earliest cases to come before the California Supreme Court in regard to school segregation occurred in 1885 in San Francisco where the plaintiff, eight-year-old Mamie Tape, the daughter of two Chinese American immigrants (Joseph and Mary) tried to enroll in San Francisco's public Spring Valley School in 1884. When Mamie was turned away from the school, her parents sued the city for violating an 1880 law that guaranteed "all children . . . residing in the district" admission to public schools. A Superior Court judge ruled that denying a child, born of Chinese parents in the state of California, entrance to the public schools would be a violation of state law and the Constitution of the United States. Mary and Joseph also argued on behalf of the right to citizenship of their American-born children and that as tax-paying residents, they had the right to have their children attend schools in their neighborhood (Wollenberg, 1978). The California Supreme Court also found in the Tapes' favor.

As a means of thwarting the court order, Mamie was denied admission again on the basis that the school was at capacity and Mamie lacked a certificate of vaccination. In order to avoid abiding by the rulings and integrating its public schools, San Francisco passed a special provision establishing separate schools for children of "Mongolian or Chinese" descent and that once those segregated schools were established the students could not be admitted to White schools. Though the Tapes won their case, the provision prevented

Mamie from attending Spring Valley, and in April 1885, she and her brother Frank became the first students of San Francisco's Chinese Primary School (Low, 1982). While school segregation has largely been discussed in history as a Black–White movement, the "separate as if equal" clause in Mamie Tape's case actually set precedence for the *Plessy v. Ferguson* case in 1896, which solidified the scope of "Jim Crow" and the "separate but equal" doctrine into public schools. Separate but equal schooling would remain in effect until it was overturned with the 1954 *Brown v. Board of Education* decision. However, as seen in the *Tape v. Hurley* case, *de facto* segregation remained rampant for more a decade until the case of *Alexander v. Holmes County Board of Education* (1969) ordered immediate desegregation rather than the previous liberally interpreted clause of desegregation "with all deliberate speed."

Aoki v. Deane (1907)

The increasing fear of the yellow peril in the schools would also affect the presence of Japanese American schoolchildren in San Francisco, where they comprised less than one tenth of 1% of the overall San Francisco Unified School District student population. Despite California's school codes for the establishment of separate schools for "Mongolians and Chinese," in essence forbidding their entry into White public schools, San Francisco's Japanese American schoolchildren attended integrated schools for a limited time (as their numbers were so few). But on the morning of January 17, 1907, 10-year-old Keikichi Aoki was denied entry at San Francisco's Redding School where Principal M. A. Deane stood guard. This test case, to determine whether San Francisco and the State of California had the right to force Japanese American children to attend segregated schools, was ultimately dismissed and settled out of court (Wollenberg, 1978). The subsequent involvement of the Japanese consulate and President Theodore Roosevelt resulted in the establishment of the 1907 Gentlemen's Agreement whereby immigration into the United States from Japan, already heavily restricted, was further curtailed. For those who already established families and communities within their ethnic enclaves, the second-generation Japanese Americans, Nisei, began to receive attention in the schools as "overachievers." In cases where Nisei attended schools with Whites, many White parents saw the threat of Asian achievement when Nisei students increasingly won the majority of scholastic awards during graduation (Wollenberg, 1978).

Sociologists have claimed that the relative academic success of Nisei in schools was part and parcel of their immigrant parents' generation, Issei, in Japan under Meiji rule where all Japanese citizens acquired eight years of schooling (Kitano, 1993). It would, as scholars maintain, be the context in which aims for academic success would be advanced. However, it is also important to note that with many other immigrant families of all races and ethnicities, education was seen as the primary avenue toward the attainment of social capital. Unaware, or perhaps blissfully ignorant, of these realities, the perceived yellow peril threat of the model minority enabled White residents in various California towns to establish separate schools. This time, segregation was not based on racial inferiority, per se, but rather on the threat to the social order of White students not attaining their "rightful" status on top of the academic (and racial) hierarchy.

Lum v. Rice (1927)

In considering the history of school segregation, the image of the South captures the imagination of the starkness between the "White" and "colored" races. Little is known, however, of where and how Asian immigrants travailed the dichotomous reality of the Black and White color line. In the Mississippi delta, Chinese immigrants settled and lived in between the bifurcated world of Jim Crow (Loewen, 1971) and fought a school segregation case that would reach the Supreme Court. The case of Lum v. Rice in 1927 was brought to the high court by Gong Lum, the father of then nine-year-old Martha Lum, who maintained that Martha had the right to attend the all-White Rosedale consolidated high school in Bolivar County. Being that they were not "colored," (interpreted to connote African Americans exclusively), and that their taxes went to pay for public schools, Lum reaffirmed equal protection under the 14th Amendment and requested that his daughter be able to attend the neighborhood school and not the designated colored school. In utilizing what was typically deemed the "common sense" definition of race, the Supreme Court held that it was perfectly acceptable to divide "educable" children into those of the pure White or Caucasian race, on the one hand, and the Brown,

Yellow, and Black races, on the other hand. Therefore, Martha Lum, of the Mongolian or yellow race, could not insist on being classified with the Whites (Loewen, 1971).

The interstitial existence of Asian Americans in the South has come to not only represent the variations of racial anomaly within a Black/White framework but also as a means to reinforce the power of whiteness when thrust upon the early Chinese, South Asian Indian, Mexican, and American Indian residents (Bow, 2010). For the example of the Chinese in the Mississippi Delta, there was no place to exist in between, despite their attempts to achieve "whiteness" in legal terms. They would remain "partly colored" (Bow, 2010). These constant marginalizations between racial entitlement and detriment, which affected Asian Americans at multiple levels of K–12 education in multiple regions of the United States, would eventually carry over into higher education throughout the 20th century.

Higher Education and Segregation

The continuous struggle over where Asian Americans fit in the larger realm of higher education was brought to bear most explicitly during World War II and the wholesale incarceration of nearly 120,000 West Coast Japanese Americans following wartime and racist hysteria after the bombing of Pearl Harbor on December 7, 1941. Due to the haste of their construction, most concentration camps were ill-equipped to provide education to Japanese Americans of all ages, and therefore many students "dropped out" of the formal education system and were unable to become re-integrated into public schools upon their release. Among those placed behind bars were college age Nisei (second-generation Japanese Americans) whose educational progress was abruptly halted. Scholars Robert O'Brien (1949), Thomas James (1987), Gary Okihiro (1999), and Allan Austin (2007) document various aspects of the organizational history and establishment of the Japanese American Relocation Council (JARC) in their efforts to assist over 4,000 students to leave concentration camps in order to complete a college degree. There have also been important moves to document the gendered nature of the experiences of the college Nisei (Ito, 2000; Matsumoto, 1984) as well as some that provide more current historiographical essays on education in the camps (Daniels, 2003).

The move away from concentration camps to college signaled recognition on the minds of certain higher education and government officials to provide opportunities to Nisei. At the same time, however, continued racist fears of a growing yellow peril, including those in Congress, inhibited the creation of a governmental agency to take the lead. President Eisenhower selected the American Friends Service Committee, the Quaker service organization, to play a lead role to create a private organization to organize and finance the project (Austin, 2007). Succumbing to the continued racial hysteria, the JARC redistributed and disbursed Nisei students to smaller regional colleges and universities primarily along the Midwest and Mid-Atlantic regions, rather than to the larger West Coast universities some had previously attended. From 1942 to 1946, the Relocation Council assisted in placing students at more than 600 schools. While in college, Nisei students were instructed to be "ambassadors of goodwill," to maintain a high degree of character, especially in academic and social affairs. In this light, the emphasis of the council in promoting its most successful students throughout the years may have worked to promote the idea and lay the foundation for the "model minority" that would come two decades later (Okihiro, 1999).

This is not to say that activism did not occur among Japanese American youth in the camps, however. There were notable instances in which Nisei and Nikkei tested the principles of democracy as they lived behind barbed wire (O'Brien, 1949). In fomenting resistance, many Japanese American youth and adults used the lessons they learned during their formative years of schooling to question the basis of their incarceration as American citizens (Tamura, 2010). Similarly, high school and college age youth resisted the type of curriculum offered in the camps, as it related to democratic citizenship, as an offense to their situation as prisoners (Yoo, 2000).

In documenting some of the more influential Asian American academics between 1920 and 1950, historian Henry Yu (2001) deftly records the influence of Robert Park's School of Sociology at the University of Chicago.

Placed in that liminal space as the "alien citizen" (Ngai, 2004), pioneering Asian American sociologists such as Rose Hum Lee and S. Frank Miyamoto worked within their limited spheres of influence to advance knowledge of Chinese and Japanese Americans, on the one hand, while still perpetuating and fetishizing the "exotic/other" formulations of Asians, on the other (Yu, 2001). With all good intentions aside, with respect to garnering acceptance of Asians into the civic imaginary, what became sustained were arguments that set the foundations for the model minority to emerge. The history of Asian Americans in higher education remains largely silent in this era and greater attention is required. Consistent throughout, however, is the effort to seek recognition as viable and legitimate members of society through exemplary demonstrations of citizenship, economic viability, and assimilation.

Asian American Demands for Equal Representation in Higher Education

The continuing efforts to seek recognition on college campuses by Asian American students climaxed during the 1960s when the larger social struggles for equal opportunities among disenfranchised populations transformed society. In the realm of higher education, the national social movements toward equality based on race, class, and gender along with the fight against communism abroad, particularly in East and Southeast Asia, promulgated college age youth to question conditions in higher education. The well-documented case of the Free Speech Movement (FSM) and Mario Salvo to the rise of the Black Panthers spoke to conditions in society which continued to stratify along class and racial lines (Rosenfeld, 2012). The FSM and the Black Panthers' rise in the Bay Area of California signaled a shift in which the West Coast became a site of major youth unrest. While those two movements did not intersect along organizational or ideological lines, they came to signify the population of insurgent intellectuals who sought to enact justice for the dispossessed.

The Free Speech Movement on the University of California, Berkeley, campus from 1963 to 1964 occurred during the time of increased conservatism in California's state politics. The risce of Ronald Reagan as the state's governor solidified the long history of Republican politics to quell anticommunist activities and subsequently all others deemed "subversive." The House Un-American Activities Committee (HUAC) was a strong force from the early to mid-20th century in identifying those elements deemed to be a threat to national security and crafted a witch-hunt to identify all those deemed to be communist sympathizers, directly and indirectly. What occurred at Berkeley and the Bay Area in the 1960s was the culmination of the domestic and international strife against those in power and those of the underclass (Rosenfeld, 2012). The university president at the time, Clark Kerr, arguably the most well-known of university presidents to date, would be caught between serving the interests of the students and university faculty in promoting intellectual freedom and preserving the political and business interests of the conservative elites (Rorabaugh, 1990). Growing constrictions on free speech and intellectual freedom, with concurrent student protests against such maneuvers, would soon collide. The rise of the Black Power movement along with other Third World movements in higher education called for increased attention to working class and minority students' interests.

The Black Panther Party was founded in Oakland, California, by Huey Newton and Bobby Seale on October 15, 1966. While the scope and details of the history of the group remain debated among scholars (Joseph, 2006), there can be no disagreement in terms of their aims to improve the lives of disenfranchised African Americans and other groups of color, albeit sometimes in unconventional ways. The group's creation of a document called the "Ten-Point Program," included the right to "Land, Bread, Housing, Education, Clothing, Justice and Peace," as well as exemption from conscription of African American men, among other demands (Joseph, 2006). In the Bay Area they helped to provide schooling opportunities and free breakfasts for neighboring school children. On college campuses, their work influenced student activists to demand for change at the administrative and curricular levels. One of the more relatively unknown aspects of the organization was being inclusive toward other minority groups (Omatsu, 2003). For example, Richard Aoki, a second-generation Japanese American, was elevated to the top ranks of the Black Panther Party while a student at UC Berkeley. Aoki was one of the founders of the Asian American Political Alliance and of the Third World

Liberation Front, a multiracial coalition of African American, Asian American, Latino, and Native American groups that led a student strike for the establishment of ethnic studies at Berkeley following the more well-known student strike at San Francisco State College (Yamamoto, 2011). Although recent scholarship raises critical questions about Aoki's life as a panther and as an FBI informant simultaneously, it perhaps bespeaks again to the type of world that Asian Americans had to straddle as part yet apart of the mainstream (Rosenfeld, 2012).

Questions of Aoki notwithstanding, the convergence of the rise of campus revolts and growing social unrest came to a head at San Francisco State College (SFSC) during the student strike in 1968–1969. The efforts to Americanize immigrant and minority groups toward a White, Anglo-Saxon Protestant ideal throughout the history of education would be met with vehement opposition by a young group of college activists who demanded that education (finally) reflect their cultural, racial, linguistic, and class backgrounds. The SFSC strike was a reflection of the larger political discourse on equal representation as well as a reaction against the growing corporate interests in shaping Clark Kerr's Master Plan for the California higher education system which tracked students of color into second-tier institutions designed for working-class jobs while elite White students were granted access to the top-tier universities and professional industries.

The 1960 Master Plan for Higher Education in California restructured the educational system to prepare a majority of students for the workforce and to meet the increasing demands and growth of the student population. Following on the heels of the 1958 National Defense Education Act (NDEA), which provided increased federal funds for courses of study emphasizing science, math, and particular foreign language fields and served in the interests of national security, Kerr's Master Plan resulted in the three-tiered system of higher education still evident today: University of California, California State University, and junior college systems. Each tier would serve targeted student populations with specialized functions with centralized governing boards to oversee the massive undertaking. The UC system would oversee the training for professions and be the sole authority in public higher education to award the doctor's degree for the top 12.5% of high school graduates (Umemoto,

1989). The state college system was to provide instruction in the liberal arts and sciences and in professions and applied fields, in addition to teacher education, for the top 33% of graduates where it had been 70% previously. The remaining eligible students would attend junior colleges to receive vocational training, general liberal arts, and courses to transfer to a four-year institution upon completion. The tightening of access through the development of more restrictive admissions requirements to higher education in California resulted in a net loss of minority student enrollment. At San Francisco State alone, African American enrollment dropped from an estimated 11% in 1960 to 3.6% by 1968 (Umemoto, 1989). These sweeping changes in education, along with the rise of a centralized, business- and political-based governance structure, mobilized student action at SFSC.

The outgrowth of the Third World Liberation Front (TWLF), the main organization to spearhead the SFSC student strike, was the culmination of various multiracial student groups and coalitions whose aims and mission were to raise awareness of oppression at home and abroad. The TWLF included members from the Mexican American Students Confederation (MASC), the Philippine-American Collegiate Endeavor (PACE), the Intercollegiate Chinese for Social Action (ICSA), and the Asian American Political Alliance (AAPA). African American students who were initially involved through the Black Student Union and the Black Panther Party were also influential in the formation of the TWLF (Umemoto, 1989). The multiracial coalition would be significant in addressing demands toward a right to education of all Third World students, a development of a School of Ethnic Area Studies, and the right to have Ethnic Studies taught and run by Third World peoples. The students' demands were met with resistance on the part of the college's administration, fearing that such demands would be tantamount to a diminished quality of education. Ironically a senior administrator for SFSC, a Japanese American professor, S. I. Hayakawa, would emerge to represent the conservative interests of the administration. Taking cues from the national stage of public protest, the TWLF and its supporters waged a protracted five-month strike—the longest student strike ever—that was met with continued resistance by the administration and local government and police officials. At its peak, the strike involved approximately 80% of the student body at SFSC and also prompted a concurrent walkout by the college's faculty in support of the TWLF demands.

In the end, the strike proved to be historic. While all the demands by the TWLF went unmet, significant gains resulted. Asian American students were at the forefront in spearheading long-lasting changes to higher education. For one, the establishment of the first School of Ethnic Studies in the nation at SFSC became the model through which elite public and private institutions, as well as many other types, would develop their own. Students of the TWLF organizations would remain instrumental in formulating curricula, evaluating courses, and hiring faculty throughout the formative years of the School of Ethnic Studies. The hiring of more minority faculty to teach these courses would also signify the gaining legitimacy of ethnic and gender studies courses as an intellectual field of study with direct connection to community and political awareness; although its presence on many college campuses still lies on the periphery of mainstream disciplines. The promise to fulfill unused special admissions slots, which would have been made available prior to the implementation of the Master Plan, would give rise to the expanding admissions opportunities for students of color, working-class students, and first-generation college attendees. Most importantly, the voices of Asian American students would no longer be silenced or ignored. The multiracial coalition of students also brought to bear the inherently unequal distribution of power in society and the world.

The 1960s and 1970s witnessed increasing efforts by student groups, and Asian Americans in particular, to change the face of higher education to reflect the changing demographics of the country. The presence of Asian Americans on college campuses began to surge in the 1970s and 1980s, doubling from 2% to 4%. In 1976, over 198,000 Asian American students attended higher education institutions at all levels and in 1988 those numbers increased to 497,000 (Lee, 2010). The decade from 1976 to 1986 witnessed the largest increase in enrollment at competitive private and public institutions where the proportion of Asian Americans in freshmen classes grew from 3.6% to 12.8% at Harvard, from 5.3% to 20.6% at MIT, from 5.7% to 14.7% at Stanford, and from 16.9% to 27.8% at Berkeley (Chan & Wang, 1991).

A major factor affecting this increase in college enrollment was a direct result of the 1965 Immigration Act. The provisions of the act gave preference to those who possessed professional skills and higher education degrees, in addition to family reunification. In terms of the Asian American population in the United States, between 1970 and 1980, the Asian American population increased from 1.5 million to 3.5 million (Hsia & Hirano-Nakanishi, 1989; Nakanishi, 1989). They would settle primarily in major urban centers where they comprised the fastest growing group at the time, which still continues to increase. The subsequent rise among Asian Americans on college campuses, especially in the 1980s, was the result of the children of the post-1965 immigrants reaching college age (Figures 5 and 6).

For various reasons that go beyond the simplistic cultural argument of innate predilection toward excellence, the parents of college age students typically viewed a higher education degree as the primary means toward social advancement. Often foreclosed from equivalent professional occupations of the home country, many Asian immigrant parents, despite their degree of educational attainment, accepted jobs incommensurate with their education and skill levels in the United States. Responses to the segmented labor market for immigrants and the desire for their offspring to achieve in the midst of inequitable conditions in the United States could certainly help to explain the motivations for seeking college degrees at the more elite institutions. While post-1965 Asian American immigrants were underemployed, they still believed that the value of a college degree would enable their children to obtain the socioeconomic mobility that they were not granted. However, conversely, these experiences of underemployed college graduates, glass ceilings, and household income levels becoming artificially inflated due to extended family cohabitation created an inaccurate picture of the needs and capabilities of Asian American students.

Evaluated on paper, Asian American college students were seen as doing equal or better than their counterparts of other races. Previous injustices were believed to have been remedied and the playing field for admissions, retention, and graduation seemed to have been leveled. However, a holistic analysis of their contextual situations revealed otherwise. The AAPI college experience, both in and out of the classroom, continued to disprove blanket assumptions

FIGURE 5
Total Enrollment in U.S. Higher Education for Blacks, Latinos, and AAPIs (1976–2005)

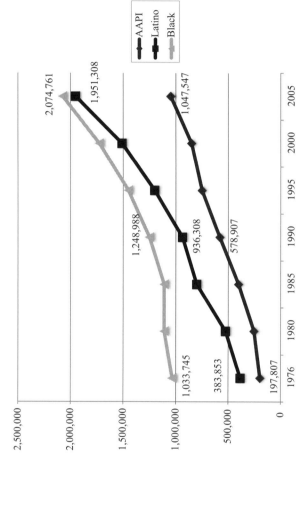

Note: Data through 1990 are for institutions of higher education, while later data are for Title IV, degree-granting institutions.
Source: Teranishi, R. T. (2010). "Analysis of data from the National Center for Education Statistics, Integrated Postsecondary Education Data Systems" (IPEDS; NCES, 2008). *Asians in the Ivory Tower* (p. 102). New York, NY: Teachers College Press. Adapted with permission.

FIGURE 6
AAPI Undergraduate Enrollment (Actual and Projected; in Thousands)

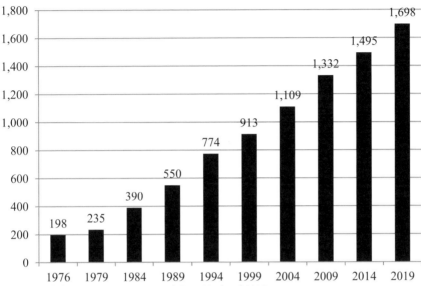

Note: Actual data, 1979–2009; projected data, 2014 and 2019.
Source: U.S. Department of Education, Common Core Data and U.S. Department of Education, IPEDS. (2011). From "The Relevance of Asian American and Pacific Islanders in the College Completion Agenda" (p. 8). *The National Commission on Asian American and Pacific Islanders Research in Education.* Adapted with permission.

of equity and excellence for this racial group. Thus, the confluence of these factors would elevate the status of AAPIs to test the limits of affirmative action admissions policies toward the turn of the century and well into the new, allegedly post-racial, millennium.

Affirmative Action and Asian American Admissions

Affirmative Action Defined

The phrase "affirmative action" was first coined by President John F. Kennedy in 1961 when he issued Executive Order 10925 that stated, in part: "The contractor will take affirmative action to ensure that applicants are employed, and that employees are treated during employment, without regard to their race, creed, color, or national origin" (Anderson, 2005, p. 114). These explicit policy measures aimed to use racial considerations in the short term, in order to remedy injustices that had been committed against people of color in the long term. Later, these proactive measures to remedy past discriminations extended to public schools, including higher education and its admissions policies. Even before "affirmative action" became part of the educational studies canon, the 1947 President's Commission on Higher Education, established by President Harry Truman, also set the stage toward a more democratic vision for higher education through its attempts to include participation by minority groups. But the realization of the plan became more visible after the passage of the various civil rights legislations of the 1960s.

In July of 1964, President Lyndon Baines Johnson signed the Civil Rights Act into law. Title VII of the act ensured protection against discrimination "based on race, color, religion, sex, or national origin" (Anderson, 2005, p. 115). The act was a direct response to institutionalized discrimination that had existed in the United States for generations in the form of antimiscegenation laws, "separate but equal" public facilities, and immigration policies that prevented a majority of immigrants from obtaining citizenship. The following year, Johnson signed Executive Order 11246, which essentially became the standing rule for affirmative action for future decades. Acknowledging the wide racial disparities in sociocultural capital and upward economic mobility that had emerged as a result of institutionalized discrimination, the government determined that proactive considerations needed to be taken in order to expedite the process of achieving racial equity. After initially addressing the disparities between African Americans and Whites, it was not until the Nixon administration when minorities became defined as "African Americans, Orientals, American Indians and persons with Spanish surnames" (Anderson, 2005, p. 117). It was based on those definitions where Asian Americans became considered for special populations categories, especially in terms of college admissions. Within a cultural and theoretical framework that saw postsecondary education emerging as the new gateway to socioeconomic mobility in the late 20th century, higher education became one of the more prominent arenas where debates about the theory and practice of affirmative action would be contested.

While affirmative action, in its original mission of bringing equity to public institutions and employment, was enacted on a widespread level, this system is not as universally utilized in higher education admissions. Across all types of colleges and universities, the vast majority of undergraduate institutions accept all qualified candidates and thus do not award special status to any group of applicants. Based on criteria such as the overall selectivity of the institution, the diversity of the applicant pool, and the desired educational outcomes established by academic administrators, only 20%–30% of higher education institutions apply some form of special admissions considerations, as it pertains to categories of race (Bowen & Bok, 1998). Understanding the complete context of affirmative action is particularly relevant for Asian Americans in higher education because a majority of Asian American college students are attending nonselective, two-year, public colleges (see Figure 7) and/or institutions that are concentrated within less than 10 states (Teranishi, 2010). As Teranishi illustrates, the idea that Asian American students are "overrepresented" at elite colleges and universities runs counter to the actual

FIGURE 7
Percent of AAPI Total Enrollment in Public Two-Year and Public Four-Year Institutions (1985–2005)

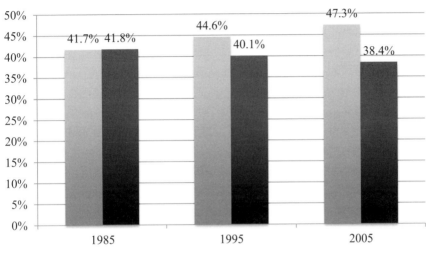

Public, Two-Year   Public, Four-Year

Source: U.S. Department of Education, IPEDS. (2011). From "The Relevance of Asian American and Pacific Islanders in the College Completion Agenda" (p. 9). *The National Commission on Asian American and Pacific Islanders Research in Education.* Adapted with permission.

data of enrolled AAPIs in postsecondary education. Much like the "Yellow Peril" stereotype of years past, it is apparent that the fear of affirmative action is not so much a quantitative issue (how many Asian Americans there are) but more so a qualitative issue (where the Asian Americans are).

While stereotypes of the model minority and yellow peril may lead people to believe that Asian Americans are overpopulating American society, the actual population demographics and educational attainment of Asian Americans tell a different story. It is only through such critical assessments of data throughout the educational system that we will be able to truly measure whether affirmative action measures are meeting their intended outcomes or even addressing the proper problems to begin with.

Affirmative Action Toward the Turn of the Century: (Re)Defining Merit

By the 1980s, an emerging generation of Asian American college students became highly visible minorities in higher education. The 1970s witnessed the rise of Asian Americans as the fastest growing minority group in undergraduate enrollment, largely as a result of the population boom that occurred shortly after the 1965 Immigration and Nationality Act (Takagi, 1998). Between 1976 and 1982, Asian American undergraduate enrollment grew 62% while Latina/o enrollment grew 32%, White enrollment grew 5%, and African American enrollment grew 1.3% (Takagi, 1998, p. 21). As 1.5- and second-generation Asian American youth reached college age, the path toward social and cultural capital became framed within higher education attainment, particularly due to the fact that a majority of these students came from college-educated households as a result of immigration policies that favored professional labor. In their pursuit of higher education, Asian Americans' new and notable presence on college campuses in the 1980s began to threaten special admissions policies not just for Asian Americans but also for all students from underrepresented populations. Critics of affirmative action contended that the burgeoning presence of Asian Americans in colleges and universities exemplified the fact that race was no longer a significant factor in one's educational experience. Thus, a new type of "yellow peril" began to surface in conjunction with the familiar trope of Asians as the overachieving "model minority." Were they targeted for being "too successful"? And were they held to a different standard in admissions that was not an accurate evaluation of their merit?

Throughout the late 20th century, two questions would begin to emerge in affirmative action discourse: (a) Do Asian Americans still need affirmative action considerations? And, (b) if Asian Americans are no longer in need of special considerations, then why isn't everyone no longer in need? Inevitably, these questions are tied to larger cultural and political debates regarding the purpose of higher education and the often zero sum determinations of whose merits were worthy enough to be granted access into selective colleges and universities. Therefore, the role of affirmative action in the college-going

TABLE 1
AAPI Enrollment in U.S. Higher Education by Institutional Type (1980–2005)

	1980	1990	2005	Change 1980–2005	Change 1990–2005
Four-year public	94,973	213,446	356,448	275.3%	67.0%
Four-year private	29,173	71,101	114,893	293.8%	61.6%
Two-year public	84,773	211,920	398,384	369.9%	88.0%

Note: Does not include four-year private for-profit institutions or two-year private not-for-profit institutions. Data for 1980 are for institutions of higher education, while data for 1990 and 2005 are for Title IV, degree-granting institutions.
Source: Teranishi, R. T. (2010). "Analysis of data from the National Center for Education Statistics, Integrated Postsecondary Education Data System" (IPEDS; NCES, 2010b). *Asians in the Ivory Tower* (p. 106). New York, NY: Teachers College Press. Adapted with permission.

process of Asian Americans must be evaluated based on the effects of affirmative action on all college students, not simply within the context of students of color, or simply in relation to Asian Americans.

Contrary to the belief of Asian American exceptionalism in higher education, Table 1 documents the biggest rate of growth occurring in the two-year public institutions. Yet the national debates of admissions and access, particularly as it affects AAPI students, continue to center on the impact of Asian Americans in elite universities. Some of the more prominent public debates over affirmative action in the 1980s took place in universities such as Brown, Harvard, Princeton, Stanford, Yale, the University of California, Berkeley, and the University of California, Los Angeles. Each of these universities was accused of discriminating against Asian Americans in their admissions decisions. Scholars Dana Takagi (Takagi, 1998), Don Nakanishi (Hsia & Hirano-Nakanishi, 1989; Nakanishi, 1989, 1993; Nakanishi & Nishida, 1995), and L. Ling-chi Wang (Chan & Wang, 1991; Wang, 1988) uncovered the hidden biases these institutions employed in discriminating against Asian American applicants, despite the institutions' denial of wrongdoing. Concurrent to these admissions scandals were ongoing debates by neoconservatives and liberals alike who pointed the finger at affirmative action policies to blame for biases against Asian Americans. The essential argument of underqualified minority students being admitted at the expense of highly qualified Asian Americans became the rally cry toward dismantling affirmative action programs. What the admissions scandals revealed was the deliberate way in which the discussion over race would become a precursor to the eventual retreat from race on college campuses (Takagi, 1998).

How administrators and policy makers began to talk about race, meritocracy, and affirmative action is a central feature of Takagi's (1998) analysis of the shifting discourse that occurred in the 1980s. Takagi contends that the Asian American admissions scandals brought to bear the centrality of AAPIs in the debate over affirmative action, where it had previously been understood as solely a "Black/White" issue. Three distinct periods characterized the changing debate throughout the 1980s. The first period, 1983–1986, defined AAPI admissions as a problem of racial discrimination when Asian Americans alleged the use of quotas and ceilings at elite universities. Critics claimed that more qualified Asian American students were not being admitted in comparison to their White counterparts. Nakanishi's (1989) explorations of the admissions controversy in the 1980s revealed that given the proportion of qualified Asian American students applying to institutions such as UCLA, UC Berkeley, and Stanford, their rate of acceptance in specific fields and disciplines (e.g., fine arts, arts and sciences, and engineering) was lower than Whites. The consistency of lower proportional acceptance rates of Asian Americans across the board at elite institutions drew the Office of Civil Rights of the U.S. Department of Education to launch the most exhaustive investigation at that time of the admissions controversy at UC Berkeley. AAPI professors, activists, and students levied charges that many elite universities set quotas on the number of admitted Asian American students. They argued that the admission rate for Asian Americans was lower than that of Whites and that the AAPI enrollment did not rise in proportion to their sharp increase in the applicant pool (Takagi, 1998). These varying levels of analysis—whether to measure student diversity in terms of raw numbers or percentages, whether to compare student body population demographics to the general population or the applicant pool, or whether to compare numbers within or across campuses, etc.—called into question what various sides' fundamental assumptions were about the endgame of affirmative action and how it might be measured. Was it, in fact, possible to use race as a central means to achieve an equitable set of circumstances where racial disparities would no longer be an issue?

In the second period, 1987–1988, university officials' responses to charges of discrimination in admissions shifted the focus of the debate to issues of overrepresentation, diversity, and meritocracy (Takagi, 1998). This period marked a pivotal change in how Asian American student applicants would be constructed. Previously viewed as victims of an unfair ceiling and quota system, university officials would now indicate that Asian American students were not holistically competitive enough to gain entry into the country's elite institutions. School officials began to invoke the idea of "diversity of experiences" as a way to explain why Asian American students were not accepted in proportion to their numbers in the overall applicant pool. In essence, Asian Americans were too studious and not star athletes, cheerleaders, nor student body presidents; their talent base was too limited to fulfill universities' visions for higher education. This notion that Asian American students were qualified but not competitive provided increasingly subjective criteria in gauging undergraduate admissions. However, the end result of Asian American underrepresentation in colleges remained the same.

In the final phase of the 1980s admissions scandals, support for Asian Americans came from an unusual ally as neoconservatives began to weigh in on their justifications for discrimination against AAPIs. In a speech at a conference on discrimination against Asian American students in higher education, Attorney General William B. Reynolds, the head of the Civil Rights Division of the U.S. Department of Justice, placed blame squarely on affirmative action policies in discriminating against Asian American applicants. In his now infamous quote he maintained, "There is substantial statistical evidence that Asian American candidates face higher hurdles than academically less qualified candidates of other races, whether those candidates be minorities (black, Hispanic, Native American) or white. . . In other words, the phenomenon of a 'ceiling' on Asian American admissions is the inevitable result of the 'floor' that has been built for a variety of other favored racial groups" (Reynolds quoted in Takagi, 1998, p. 104). In his near clarion call to dismantle affirmative action programs, Reynolds gained support from both liberals and conservatives. The move toward advancing individual merit would position Asian American students closer to an "honorary White" racial status while simultaneously widening the gap between Whites and other people of color. Such attitudes reflected a larger paradigm shift in the way that higher education would be viewed going into the 21st century. Rather than pursuing higher education as a means to achieve a public good, the costs and benefits of the college experience would become evaluated for their private benefits to the individuals who attended these institutions.

It is important here to recognize how the process of Asian American "deminoritization" in higher education (Lee, 2006) works to reinforce both the yellow peril and model minority stereotypes. They exist along a continuum that reinforces the threat of Asian overrepresentation while lauding high academic achievement (Ng et al., 2007). This narrow viewpoint of the Asian American educational experience became the accepted way of constructing affirmative action in efforts to abolish it altogether, rather than amending it to address shifts in the demographics of specific groups (Poon, 2009a, 2009b). Completely lost among these debates was any sort of holistic analysis about the causes and effects of affirmative action. Asian Americans, assumed to be the model minority, were categorized as the all-deserving exception to the rule. Blacks and Latinos, on the other hand, assumed to be the antithesis of the model minority, were demonized as undeserving freeloaders who were gaining unfair handouts.

Negative Action Versus Affirmative Action

The configuration of Asian American students in the affirmative action debate since the late 1970s points to the growing public perception that Asian Americans have been hurt by affirmative action policies (Poon, 2009a, 2009b). The typical trope was that their cultural values of hard work and achievement through individual merit worked against them in a social system that rewarded those with lesser qualifications. Devoid of the deeper contextual and historical remnants of the development of affirmative action policies, political conservatives and liberals would ally themselves to a cause of touting Asian values toward a culture of achievement. This static and monolithic view of

Asian culture's proclivity toward high academic achievement started to work against African Americans and Latina/os. The scenario was thus laid out that AAPI students' denial into elite institutions was due to affirmative action policies that benefited lesser qualified students. In tracing this particular public discourse, legal scholar Jerry Kang (1996) came to identify the concept of "negative action" versus affirmative action at the crux of this debate. Kang defines negative action as "unfavorable treatment based on race, using the treatment of Whites as a basis for comparison. In functional terms, negative action against Asian Americans is in force if a university denies admission to an Asian American who would have been admitted had that person been White" (Kang, 1996, p. 3).

The admissions scandals at elite universities in the 1980s were essentially based on negative action against AAPI applicants wherein their chance of being admitted was less than an equally qualified White applicant. Negative action is distinct from affirmative action policies as "plus factors" are provided to some African American, Latina/o, and American Indian applicants (Kidder, 2005). Negative action then occurs when a "minus factor" is applied to AAPI candidates in relation to their White counterparts. This is a practice that is separate and apart from any affirmative action "plus factors" given to under-represented minorities such as African Americans, Latina/os, and American Indians in the admissions process (Kang, 1996; Kidder, 2005). The conflation between negative action and affirmative action became a way to provide a simplistic view of why affirmative action was wrong. Thus, providing preference to African Americans, Latinos, and American Indians was predicated on Asian Americans losing out in disproportionate numbers. The zero sum game of college admissions meant that someone would inevitably lose out. However, the improper conflation of negative and affirmative action creates the misconception of who "loses" out and why.

In a highly publicized study investigating the possible effects of eliminating affirmative action policies in admissions, Espenshade and Chung (2005) predicted that the greatest beneficiaries would be Asian American applicants, in that "they would occupy four out of every five seats created by accepting fewer African American and Hispanic students" (p. 304) and that increase in White applicants would be inconsequential. Despite the empirical problematics embedded within the "yellow peril causation fallacy" (Kidder, 2005) the authors advance, prominent voices in higher education also echoed similar sentiments. Asian Americans would enter the ivory towers in throngs and be yet another horde of invaders. In realistic terms, the eradication of affirmative action policies in states such as California, Washington, and Michigan and entrance into the top law schools in the nation witnessed fluctuations in AAPI enrollments (Kidder, 2005). The threat of the yellow peril causation fallacy did not happen. What did occur on a more expansive scale was the diminishing rate of African American and Latina/o students in those institutions where affirmative action policies were abolished. But what continued to remain were concerns over the rise of Asian American admissions, as opposed to a more holistic evaluation regarding the effects of affirmative action on all applicants. Eventually, these concerns regarding affirmative action would find their way to the highest courts of the American judicial system on multiple occasions over the last four decades. Cases such as *Regents of the University of California v. Bakke* (1978), which denied the explicit use of racial quotas, and *Grutter v. Bollinger* (2003), which allowed for race to be used as a narrowly tailored means to pursue a compelling state interest in diversity, set guidelines for affirmative action which continue to be contested to the present day through the current Supreme Court case of *Fisher v. University of Texas* (2013).

The Model Minority Goes to Court: The Impact of *Bakke, Gratz, Grutter,* and *Fisher*

As has been the case with innumerable race-based public policies throughout the years, affirmative action in college admissions has been shaped by resistance in the form of legal action, which used the courts as a means to debate the practice of ambiguous and questionable laws. However, in contrast to previous challenges to voting rights, antimiscegenation, and Jim Crow, the public face of resistance to affirmative action policies in higher education admissions has been universally White. Most notably, four cases relating to affirmative action have been argued all the way to the U.S. Supreme Court: *Regents of the University of California v. Bakke* (1978), *Gratz v. Bollinger* (2003),

Grutter v. Bollinger (2003), and *Fisher v. University of Texas* (2013). In accordance with the natural flow of legal precedent, each of these cases' individual rulings has had a snowball effect on subsequent issues of affirmative action and racial representation in higher education and beyond. Furthermore, each case's political context has been shaped by the constantly evolving racial dynamics of the United States.

Allan Bakke's case against the University of California arose from his denial to the medical school at the University of California at Davis. Bakke argued that his denial was unconstitutional because the university set aside a fixed number of seats in its medical school for "disadvantaged students." The Supreme Court ruled that a quota system, which set aside a fixed number of admissions for students, went beyond the scope of affirmative action, and Bakke was admitted to the medical school at UC Davis. However, the court still maintained that affirmative action policies would be permissible so long as strict quotas were not implemented. Twenty-five years later, two cases were brought against the University of Michigan as Jennifer Gratz and Barbara Grutter both filed suits claiming discrimination in the university's admissions criteria at the undergraduate and law school levels, respectively. The ruling in the *Gratz* case determined that categorically rewarding racial/ethnic minorities 20 points on an admissions criteria scale was unconstitutional. This ruling echoed sentiments of *Bakke*, which seemed to award "plus" factors to applicants based on race alone rather than some combination of race and academic merit. However, the university's affirmative action admissions procedure for its law school was upheld in the *Grutter* case, as the Supreme Court ruled that the considerations of race in that instance were narrowly tailored toward pursuing and achieving the specific educational goal of diversity.

The turnaround time before affirmative action in higher education re-entered the legal system's largest stage was far shorter after the *Grutter* and *Gratz* rulings. In 2008, after having her undergraduate application to the University of Texas at Austin denied, Abigail Fisher filed suit. Believing that her academic credentials exceeded those of many minority student applicants who were admitted to the university, she sought injunctive relief barring the university's consideration of race in admissions, the re-evaluation of her application absent of racial considerations, and refunds of her application fees. By 2012, the case reached the U.S. Supreme Court, around the same time that Fisher completed a bachelor's degree at Louisiana State University.

The sociopolitical context of Abigail Fisher's case is noteworthy for multiple reasons. First, the landmark case that desegregated higher education, *Sweatt v. Painter* (1950), also took place at the same campus—the University of Texas at Austin. The flagship public university of the second biggest state in the union once again found itself at the forefront of race relations in higher education. Furthermore, the case came to prominence during an era when the election of President Barack Obama raised more skepticism than ever regarding whether or not institutional racism still exists in the United States. The case also raised many questions about the endgame of diversity. How do we know when it has been achieved? How can progress be measured? Arguments from Abigail Fisher contended that the university's "Ten Percent Rule," which granted automatic admissions for the top 10% of students from each Texas public high school, was able to achieve the goal of diversifying the campus without considering race explicitly. However, the university countered that the rampant segregation that occurred in the K–12 system still perpetuated race- and class-based stratification that should be considered when evaluating applicants. Ultimately, the case was not ruled upon by the Supreme Court but remanded to the Fifth Circuit United States Court of Appeals. The Supreme Court determined that the lower court did not sufficiently rule on whether or not the university passed a strict scrutiny test of narrowly tailored means toward a compelling interest.

While the new ruling of the lower court is still under consideration, the amicus briefs from the *Fisher* case provide insight into the positioning of Asian American students in the current affirmative action discourse. For after five decades of debates on affirmative action, it has become clear that communities of color themselves are highly divided on the issue. The consideration of race is no longer simply an issue of the White majority versus racial minorities. Rather, it has also become a very prevalent topic of discussion within racial and ethnic groups. Within the Asian American community, the *Fisher* case has exemplified these debates in both academic- and community-based environments.

Affirmative Action in Contemporary Asian America

In addition to the arguments filed by both parties in the *Fisher v. University of Texas* case, Asian Americans have submitted amicus curiae briefs to the Court in support of both parties. The individuals and entities who have authored these briefs are civil rights groups, nonprofit organizations, professional organizations, and university student organizations, staff, and faculty (including those from the University of Texas at Austin itself) who all purport to have a direct connection to and extensive knowledge of the Asian American community. Six amicus curiae briefs (three in support of each party) that name Asian Americans as primary authors uncover many similar debates that have occurred throughout history regarding the role of Asian American students within the higher education landscape; except this time, the philosophical oppositions have distinctly divided the Asian American community. The arguments made within these briefs illustrate fundamental philosophical differences among AAPIs regarding the definition of diversity, the privileges and disadvantages of adopting "Asian American" as a racial category, and the role of higher education as a catalyst to facilitate social mobility.

Amicus curiae briefs in support of Abigail Fisher support the Petitioner's argument that the University of Texas' consideration of race has a negative effect on Asian Americans by allowing lesser qualified students to gain admissions seats which, absent of racial considerations, would have been awarded to Asian Americans. All three briefs in support of Fisher point to statistics, which illustrate a wide discrepancy in standardized test scores and GPAs between Asian Americans and African Americans and Latinos, who are considered underrepresented minorities by the University of Texas. Statistics compiled by Espenshade and Radford (2009) are cited by all three amicus briefs. Espenshade and Radford's study of the admissions process at three private universities concluded that Asian American students had to have an SAT score of approximately 140 points higher than Whites in order to gain an equivalent chance of admission. However, Black and Hispanic applicants with SAT scores that were respectively 310 and 130 points lower than Whites were also determined to have an equivalent chance of admission (Brief for AALF as

Amicus Curiae in Support of Petitioner, p. 12). Thus, Asian Americans in support of Abigail Fisher believe that eliminating race from consideration in college admissions is the only rational solution to remedy these inequities in a process that is supposed to be objective and merit based.

The 80–20 National Asian American Educational Foundation (80–20), in identifying its interests as an amicus in the case, purports its own survey of 47,000 participants which concluded that Asian Americans supported race-neutral, merit-based college admissions by a ratio of 52:1 (Brief *Amicus Curiae* of LDB, 80–20, et al., in Support of Petitioner, p. 2). The brief filed by 80–20 in conjunction with the Louis D. Brandeis Center for Human Rights Under Law (LDB), the National Federation of Indian American Associations, the Indian American Forum for Political Education, and the Global Organization of People of Indian Origin emphasizes the argument that Asian Americans are the "new Jews" of college admissions. 80–20 and their fellow amici argue that the current holistic admissions policy proposed by the University of Texas is the latest in a lineage of highly subjective admissions criteria that have been used to deny admissions to students whom institutions deemed undesirable. They draw parallels between the rationale used to covertly exclude Jews from colleges in the early 20th century and the rhetoric which is currently being used to promote affirmative action in order to illustrate that well-intentioned people who believe to be acting in the best interest of others are not exempt from perpetuating gross injustices (Brief *Amicus Curiae* of LDB, 80–20, et al., in Support of Petitioner, pp. 20–33).

The concept of state accountability in practices of racial considerations is also addressed by the Asian American Legal Foundation (AALF) in two separate amicus briefs—one filed as a single entity and one filed in conjunction with the Judicial Education Project (JEP). The amicus briefs submitted by the AALF contend that without strict scrutiny, race-conscious policies can devolve into racial balancing for the sake of racial balancing rather than a narrowly tailored means to pursue a compelling state interest. In agreement with the amicus brief of the LDB and 80–20, the AALF argues that such subjective criteria are used to mask the blatant political favoritism of some racial/ethnic groups over others (Brief for AALF and JEP as *Amicus Curiae* in Support of Petitioner, pp. 2–5). Furthermore, the AALF believes that judicial deference to the schools could have a trickledown effect on public education through the K–12 system. Citing the case of *Ho v. San Francisco Unified School District* (1998), AALF argues that racial balancing at any level of education does not contribute to a more productive educational experience, but rather stigmatizes race, denigrates students' self-esteem, and promotes dishonesty among self-reported racial classifications (Brief of AALF as *Amicus Curiae* in Support of Petitioner, pp. 13–15).

The briefs filed in support of Abigail Fisher take the stance that the consideration of race-based admissions will inevitably corrupt the admissions system, stripping it of its objective criteria (test scores, GPAs, etc.) and placing more emphasis on highly subjective notions of what connotes a "competitive" applicant. These amici further argue that true diversity can only be evaluated on an individual level, not by assigning people to racial categories. In response, the amicus briefs filed in support of the university directly oppose those filed in support of Fisher through their emphasis on the use of racial considerations amid a holistic educational process, analysis of statistics regarding Asian American achievement, purported scope and objectives of diversity, and the onus placed on the state to pursue compelling interests.

An amicus brief filed by a collective named the Coalition of Bar Associations of Color offers a long-term outlook on the role of higher education in perpetuating a just society. Coauthored by the National Bar Association (an African American bar association), the Hispanic National Bar Association, the National Asian Pacific Bar Association, and the National Native American Bar Association, this coalition argues that progress should not be conflated with success. Although underrepresented racial and ethnic minority populations have matriculated into higher education, people of color are still grossly underrepresented in law schools and at all levels of the legal profession (Brief of *Amici Curiae* Coalition of Bar Associations of Color in Support of Respondents, pp. 7–9). The coalition maintains the belief that a diverse population of justices, lawyers, and policy makers is crucial toward the perpetuation of a society that is committed to justice for all its citizens. Their brief highlights what they believe is a fundamental irony of the legal profession by quoting a Stanford Law professor who wrote, "One irony of this nation's continuing struggle for diversity and gender equity in employment is that the profession leading the struggle has failed to set an example in its own workplaces" (Brief of *Amici Curiae* Coalition of Bar Associations of Color in Support of Respondents, p. 22). Furthermore, the amici also emphasize the direct connection between the legal profession and high levels of government leadership, citing that 25 U.S. presidents have been lawyers, and they are also currently the largest occupational group in Congress (Brief of *Amici Curiae* Coalition of Bar Associations of Color in Support of Respondents, pp. 14–15). Given that the legal field is strictly dependent on post-graduate higher education as a job qualification, the Coalition of Bar Associations of Color sees undergraduate admissions as an important beginning point to foster diversity that they believe is invaluable to governmental interests. This idea that the interests of public universities go far beyond the physical space of their campus or their student body is also reflected through the other briefs which support the University of Texas.

The Asian American Center for Advancing Justice ("Advancing Justice"), in its amicus brief coauthored with over 70 additional nonprofit, professional, civil rights, and student organizations, argues that diversity in higher education and the workplace is beneficial to all people, not just racial and ethnic minorities. Advancing Justice also addresses the lack of Asian American leadership in the workforce and several academic fields and argues that holistic review of applicants inclusive of racial considerations is crucial in developing leadership from populations that contribute a wider spectrum of experiences (Brief of *Amici Curiae* Advancing Justice, et al., in Support of Respondents, p. 4). Furthermore, the development of diverse leadership is reciprocal in that it allows all students, whether from traditionally underrepresented population demographics or not, to learn from a more diverse peer group and also normalize viewing and accepting more types of people as potential leaders. This mutually beneficial system of diversity is crucial in making all students competitive and successful in the professional marketplace (Brief of *Amici Curiae*. Advancing Justice, et al., in Support of Respondents, pp. 18–22). The brief of Advancing Justice also directly rebuts the survey cited by 80–20 by citing formal voting patterns and alternative surveys of Asian Americans in regards to race-conscious public policies (Brief of *Amici Curiae* Advancing Justice, et al., pp. 2–3). This use of alternative statistical analysis and interpretation is applied throughout briefs in support of the university, as many amici question the validity of Fisher's arguments about achievement gaps among both applicant pools and student bodies.

The briefs filed by Advancing Justice and the Asian American Legal Defense and Education Fund (AALDEF) also dedicate a majority of their arguments to the notion of Asian Americans and "negative action," or the belief that the consideration of race puts Asian Americans at a distinct disadvantage for admissions by negating their objective qualifications on account of racial preferences. The AALDEF brief, which is coauthored with over 1,000 fellow amici, directly attacks the argument about the racial qualifications gap by illustrating that these inequities have existed for the past two decades, regardless of whether universities have implemented race-conscious admissions. Therefore, these inconsistencies are more so the result of educational inequities rather than selective college admissions. The AALDEF also illustrates that Asian American applicants and students are concentrated in the academic fields which are most competitive to begin with, thus also accounting for the discrepancy in test scores and GPAs (Brief of the AALDEF, et al., in Support of Respondents, pp. 18–23). In dialogue with these discussions about the value of standardized testing in establishing well-qualified candidates, the amicus brief of Advancing Justice also notes that SAT scores are not directly correlated with long-term academic success, thus further supporting a system of holistic review which measures candidates on their potential contributions to the campus climate and workforce (Brief of *Amici Curiae* Advancing Justice, et al., in Support of Respondents, pp. 29–34).

Going more in-depth to the University of Texas at Austin's population as a direct example, the AALDEF and Advancing Justice rebut the labeling of Asian Americans as "overrepresented." Using data from the entire post-*Hopwood* era, which as of the writing of these briefs encompassed six years without racial considerations and six years with them, AALDEF and Advancing Justice show that Asian American enrollment has remained relatively steady regardless of whether or not race has been utilized as a factor in admissions. The proportion of Asian American students, which has floated between 17% and 20% of the overall student population, is almost five times greater than the Asian American population of the state of Texas, which is approximately 4%. Therefore, the numbers proposed by the university's amicus briefs are used to refute the claims made by Fisher's amici that the University of Texas is attempting to maliciously control the number of Asian American students by giving their admissions seats to undeserving members of other racial and ethnic groups (Brief *Amicus Curiae* of Advancing Justice, et al., in Support of Respondents, pp. 26–28; Brief of AALDEF, et al. as *Amici Curiae* in Support of Respondents, pp. 11–18). These interpretations of the data reflect a grounded approach to the University of Texas at Austin's policy, which is used to contest the claims made by Abigail Fisher's amici that subjective criteria are inherently flawed and can easily be manipulated to the disadvantage of Asian Americans.

The fundamental opposition between the arguments supporting Abigail Fisher and those supporting the University of Texas at Austin is most poignantly observed in the ways that both sides channel the image of the model minority myth. The amici who support Fisher argue that the model minority myth is perpetuated by the university's consideration of race. True diversity, they argue, should only be considered on an individual level and not in terms of racialized identities (Brief for the AALF and JEP as *Amicus Curiae* in Support of Petitioner, pp. 4–5). On the contrary, the amici who support the University of Texas argue that the model minority myth can be debunked by the university's admissions policy because it considers a myriad of factors from an applicant's background other than merely race. These additional factors can go beyond the model minority myth and account for the various levels of diversity within the Asian American category (Brief of AALDEF, et al., as *Amici Curiae* in Support of Respondents, pp. 25–30). Collectively, these amici from the Asian American community reflect the diverse opinions on the issue of Asian Americans' relationship to affirmative action and the innumerable social, political, and economic interests that are rooted in postsecondary education. These concerns illustrate the emphasis that these individuals as parents, citizens, and professionals place on history, the trust they place in the hands of state institutions to be accountable to their constituents, their ideals of democracy and meritocracy, and most importantly the cost and value they assign to the field of higher education as Asian Americans.

Potential Implications of the *Fisher* Ruling

While the remand of the *Fisher* case brought the heated battle to a rather anticlimactic ending, the long-term effects of the *Fisher* ruling are also as thoroughly debated as the case itself. The United States Department of Education has emphasized that the ruling, as it currently stands, does not overturn the University of Texas's admissions policy, nor does it categorically negate the use of race as a special consideration for college applicants. It remains to be seen which colleges and universities will use the current *Fisher* ruling as a precedent, and which ones will simply continue forward with race-based considerations thinking that they will pass the test of strict scrutiny where the University of Texas did not. Furthermore, the upcoming Supreme Court case of *Schuette v. Coalition to Defend Affirmative Action* (2013) is seeking to overturn the state of Michigan's Proposition 2, which banned affirmative action in 2003. With the racial dynamics of the United States continuing to diversify, it is safe to assume this issue will be prevalent for decades to come.

The *Fisher* case has captured the attention of policymakers nationwide, questioning educational philosophies and political identities in new ways that were not as critically addressed in previous affirmative action cases. In the debate regarding the establishment of a critical mass of underrepresented students, both Abigail Fisher and the University of Texas reveal their conflicting ideals about the overall purpose of the university and its relationship to the state. In the eyes of the Fisher, being subject to race-based considerations should only be toward the objective of being accepted into the university. The university, on the other hand, views these considerations as part of an overall process which goes beyond admissions into the enrollment (which they also emphasize is a different statistic than admissions), retention, and graduation of students into a diverse citizenry and workforce. On the one hand, Abigail Fisher purports a vision of the university as a self-sufficient institution whose sole purpose is to grant students an objective opportunity to pursue a meritocratic, individual education. The University of Texas at Austin, on the other hand, believes the university has an obligation to remedy past injustices that disparately affected specific populations and continue to do so in various ways. Addressing these perpetual inequities is an integral aspect of inculcating citizens who will support the prosperity of their state in the long term.

What has gone largely ignored in the discussions surrounding this case is how the Supreme Court decision of the *Fisher v. University of Texas* will reflect larger institutional philosophies by the University of Texas at Austin as a complete educational institution, and not merely a clearinghouse for the academic elite. The arguments made by Abigail Fisher, the University of Texas at Austin, and their supporting amici focus mainly on what could happen to students before and after their tenure at the campus in question as a result of considering race as a factor in admissions. Yet these discussions inherently take for granted that the time students spend within the university, once admitted, will be universally beneficial. Completely absent from arguments about critical mass, narrowly tailored methods, and compelling state interests is an exploration of how flagship universities like the University of Texas at Austin will work to promote diversity through faculty training, student affairs, and continued academic research. The residual effects of the decision in this case should not merely be looked at as an endgame to the affirmative action debates, but should also be continuously analyzed for their relevance to practices and policy development that benefit all students, regardless of their racial/ethnic background. Only then will this principle of "holistic review" truly live up to its name and establish a foundation to work toward a truly legitimate end point.

In the fourth chapter, we provide more specific details of the range of college students' experiences that begins to provide a more accurate portrait of who the AAPIs are on college campuses. By going beyond the heavily contested battleground of college admissions, an evaluation of the qualitative experiences of AAPIs on college campuses determines whether higher education is able to deliver on the promises that it makes to students.

Influential Factors in the Asian American and Pacific Islander College Student Experience

RELATIVE TO THE LITERATURE ON UNDERSERVED popula-
tions in college, the literature on the experience of AAPI students at the
higher education level has begun to reflect a myriad of complex issues and concerns faced by this population. By the same token, despite these initial gains
in diversifying the field of educational research, the literature continues to be
limited in relation to the true diversity of AAPI student experiences throughout the higher education pipeline. Notwithstanding, the following chapter investigates the extant literature on the collegiate experiences of AAPI students
and makes recommendations for building upon current foundations. This
chapter is initially divided into these seminal aspects of higher education that
have influenced AAPI collegiate experiences: (a) campus climate, (b) identity
development, (c) family and intergenerational concerns, (d) mental health,
(e) leadership and involvement, (f) college choice, and (g) community college. Then, once our review of these subsections of higher education literature
establishes the current needs and capabilities of Asian American and Pacific
Islander students, we shift our focus toward emerging areas of research in the
study of Asian American educational experiences—growing disparities in institutional enrollment, the emergence of Asian American and Native American Pacific Islander–Serving Institutions (AANAPISIs) to explore the continuously evolving relationship between Asian American students and academia.

As mentioned earlier in this volume, researchers emphasize the importance of disaggregating data in order to have a better understanding of AAPI subgroups (Chang & Kiang, 2002; Hune, 2002; Maramba, 2011b; Museus & Chang, 2009; Teranishi, 2010; Yeh, 2004). National reports discuss the importance of the disaggregation as a starting point for effective interventions for particular AAPI populations. Disaggregating the AAPI population reveals that this category comprises over 48 ethnic groups (as noted in the first chapter; CARE, 2010). Furthermore, in addition to the ethnic diversity of the AAPI group, disaggregation of data through factors such as gender, immigration status, and socioeconomic status provides a clearer picture of the diverse educational needs that exist among Asian Americans and Pacific Islanders. Multiple, concurrent axes of disaggregated analysis illustrate the large disparities of college preparation, access, retention, and educational satisfaction among AAPI students. For example, in the case of Southeast Asian Americans (SEAAs) namely Vietnamese, Cambodian, Hmong, Lao, and Vietnamese, understanding their educational access and attainment provides a clearer picture of the disparities compared to the national average and their AAPI counterparts (Maramba, 2011b). According to Teranishi (2010), SEAAs obtaining a bachelor of arts or higher is disproportionately low compared to the 25.9% national average (Hmong, 7.5%; Cambodian, 9.2%; Lao, 7.7%; and Vietnamese, 19.4%). These populations are also more likely to attend a community college after high school compared to other AAPI ethnic groups and are less likely than their AAPI counterparts to obtain a degree (Laotians, 49.2%; Cambodians, 48.2%; Hmong, 45.5%; and Vietnamese, 36.7%; CARE, 2010). Chang, Park, Lin, Poon, and Nakanishi (2007) also explain that SEAAs are more likely to need more financial support than their AAPI counterparts. These statistics are examples of the continued need to examine AAPI subgroups more closely for a clearer picture of gaps and disproportionate educational access and attainment in higher education.

Campus Climate

The following section will cover the literature that discusses AAPIs' general college experience and perceptions of campus climate. The extant literature on

AAPIs in college indicates a strong call for more critical research that addresses their overall college experience, which includes understanding their social and academic well-being and adjustment to the college environment. More specifically, Asian American educational researchers emphasize that Asian American college students are indeed a growing and diverse population (Chang et al., 2007; Gloria & Ho, 2003; Hune, 2002; Yeh, 2002, 2004). Therefore, with the increasing diversity comes the importance of understanding the various challenges that AAPI populations may experience which are specific to an educational context that goes far beyond simple racial classifications. For example, Yeh (2002) explains that there are a number of issues and factors that influence their college experience and put AAPI college students at high educational risk. These issues include individual, family, classroom, school, and community concerns. Wang et al. (2009), who studied Asian American community college students, suggest that addressing community-wide levels of schooling, English proficiency, and academic goal setting are important elements in effectively serving this population. By having a better understanding of how risk factors influence AAPI college experiences, institutions can more efficiently refine their recruitment and retention efforts toward the specific needs of this population. However, perhaps the most salient issue in AAPI's college experience is the way in which they perceive the campus racial climate. The following discusses the existing literature relevant to the AAPI perceptions of campus racial climate.

Hurtado and associates have discussed the importance of universities to produce elements that will positively affect the racial climate for students of color (Hurtado, Milem, Clayton-Pedersen, & Allen, 1999; Milem, Clayton-Pedersen, Hurtado, & Allen, 1998). Among those elements, they suggest considering various context and dimensions such as the historical legacy of inclusion/exclusion, structural diversity, psychological climate, and behavioral dimensions to create an inclusive environment. A comprehensive study of campus racial climates for students of color shows that environments have yet to be more comfortable for ethnic minority students (Harper & Hurtado, 2007). Notwithstanding, these are useful and informative studies for a better understanding of campus racial climates; however, these studies have also indicated that various racial and ethnic groups experience the college campus differently. This is true in the case of AAPIs. Studies reveal that the AAPI population has shown low satisfaction levels and experiences their college environment differently from their college counterparts. For example, Einarson and Clarkberg (2010) explain that Asian Americans who were dissatisfied overall with their college experience were those least likely to interact with faculty compared to their racial counterparts. In addition, Ancis et al. (2000) and Einarson and Matier (2005) show that Asian Americans and African Americans are the least satisfied in the college experience compared to their peers. Similarly, Asian Americans had only slightly higher satisfaction levels with the campus racial climate than their Black counterparts (Museus, 2008). Correspondingly, a national study of undergraduates shows that the Asian American population is more likely to be satisfied with a racially diverse environment when they attend an institution that is more diverse (Park, 2009).

In response to the current trends in perceptions of campus climate, researchers have indicated that it is vital that the study of campus climates be more closely examined especially with regard to specific Asian American ethnic groups and using various methodologies, which not only assess the needs of students but also their strengths. Despite these findings of low levels of satisfaction with campus climate, specifically in relation to race, other research has also discovered the ways in which Asian American students have utilized their own social networks as a means of coping with institutional and interpersonal racism and offering forms of resistance. Gloria and Ho (2003), who examined Chinese, Filipino, Japanese, Korean, Pacific Islander, and Vietnamese Americans, suggest that perceived social support systems such as family and friends are strongly associated with contributing to AAPIs' positive academic college experience. Furthermore, Maramba and Museus (2011) explain that the use of mixed methods, that is, qualitative and quantitative approaches, is vital in expanding our understanding of racial climates for Filipino Americans. In particular, they contend that the sense of belonging to Filipino Americans is very much intertwined with their sense of belonging to the campus (Maramba & Museus, 2011, 2012; Museus & Maramba, 2011). Moreover, there are a number of factors that must be addressed with regard to the academic and social college environment such as college curriculum, student services, and social interactions that facilitate a more comfortable learning environment

(Maramba, 2008b). Likewise, cultural validation on and off campus is also an important component in facilitating successful college experiences of Southeast Asian American students (Maramba & Palmer, in press). In their study of Cambodian American students, Chhuon and Hudley (2008) stress that the presence of a Cambodian club and involvement with a program that connected them with faculty assisted in their successful adjustment. Such services were particularly relevant to this immigrant refugee population as an overwhelming majority of Cambodian American students are the first in their families to attend college in either the United States or Cambodia. These varied experiences of Asian American subgroups illustrate then that campus climate is not just about what the university can provide the students, but also what the students bring to the university. By approaching campus climate as a two-way dialogue rather than a one-way path to success and development, student services practitioners can help to create a holistic educational experience that will enable students to develop as both students and members of their communities.

Identity Development

As is the case with all young adults, identity development in all its nuanced aspects is a significant aspect of students' lives. The literature on Asian American identity is largely examined via the development of racial and ethnic identity (Alvarez, 2002; Kim, 2001). More specific to Asian American college students, existing racial identity frameworks have been presented by examining a pan-ethnic Asian American model. Overall, racial identity has also been positively correlated with collective self-esteem as part of the pan-ethnic Asian American group (Alvarez & Helms, 2001). For example, Alvarez (2002) used Helm's People of Color racial identity model to examine the racial identity of Asian American students. Alvarez (2002) explainss that they may experience distinct stages of identity development, which include conformity, dissonance, immersion/emersion, internalization, and integrative awareness wherein the main emphasis is to assist student affairs practitioners understand the various stages that Asian Americans might experience their racial and ethnic identity. Another model that provides a more direct application to student affairs is Jean Kim's (2001) Asian American Identity Development

Model, which outlines the stages of ethnic awareness, White identification, awakening to social/political consciousness, redirection to Asian American consciousness, and incorporation. The connotations of each of these stages provide a blueprint for directing programming geared toward student interests and experiences past, present, and future. They also imply the sense of collectivity that is inherent in identity formation. One's identity does not exist in a vacuum but is constantly in dialogue with others who are both internal and external to one's identity and community.

Other perspectives include understanding Asian American identity on a psychosocial development level. In the psychosocial development model, the main premise lies in the integration of context and U.S. societal external influences and Asian traditional values (Kodama, McEwen, Liang, & Lee, 2002). Central to this model are categories of identity and purpose, which serve as the foundations for other developmental areas as emotions, competency, interdependence, relationships, and integrity. On a similar level, Kawaguchi (2003) explains that there are four distinct patterns of Asian American ethnic identity development: achieved, moratorium, foreclosed, and diffuse. More importantly, the awareness of one's experience as a minority, the link to the Asian model minority myth, and the strong connection between ethnicity and their chosen academic field or career were found to have direct connections with each other (Kawaguchi, 2003). Additionally, Kodama and Abreo (2009) found that with regard to ethnic and racial identity preference, college students tended to identify with either their ethnic (exclusively referring to their ancestral homeland) or ethnic American ("hyphenated") identities.

To address the diversity of Asian American groups, a number of researchers have discussed ethnic identity development models relative to specific Asian ethnic groups (Ibrahim, Ohnishi, & Sandhu, 1997; Kibria, 1999; Museus, Maramba, Palmer, Reyes, & Bresonis, 2013; Nadal, 2004; Wong, 2013). Chinese and Korean Americans, with regard to the "private" and "public" aspects of identity formation, felt stifled by what they felt to be an artificial Asian American social category and preferred ethnic group identification (Kibria, 1999). These narrative accounts of students' attitudes toward the Asian American identity reflect the social construction of race and constant fluidity of racial identities. Similarly, Nadal (2004) placed emphasis on the historical, sociocultural, and acculturation levels in context for Filipino American identity. Within Pakistani and Indian American cultural identity, Ibrahim et al. (1997) also examined identity within social, psychological, cultural, and political context of the Indian culture within the United States. Each of these models points to the diverse heterogeneity within the Asian American category and thus cautions educational professionals to consider the specific material conditions that surround Asian Americans in both historical and contemporary settings.

Beyond race and ethnicity, the intersecting relationships between gender, sexuality, and racial identity of Asian Americans in educational environments have also been explored, as this issue is becoming increasingly salient for many researchers of student development and identity formation across the board. Asian American studies' scholars have extensively documented the bifurcated gender stereotypes of Asian Americans, which characterize males as asexual nerds and females as hypersexualized "dragon ladies" (Hong, 2011; Ono & Pham, 2008; Parrenas-Shimizu, 2007, 2012). For Asian American men, a higher cognitive awareness of discrimination, both racially and on a gendered level, is negatively related to self-esteem (Shek & McEwen, 2012). Within the frame of an Asian American gay, lesbian, and bisexual (GLB) identity, Narui (2011) explain GLB students' "double minority" status and that the identity is based on a student's perception of her/his environment on a macro and micro level (e.g., university versus classroom and community versus residence hall) rather than a linear identity progression that evolves from a state of tragic dissonance to a state of universal acceptance. Pepin & Talbot (2013) also discuss the constant negotiation between students who identify as Asian American and as a gay, lesbian, or bisexual. They further explained that they did not always want their two identities to intersect but that it was evident that they often negotiated their dueling identities. This fluctuation of identities based on environmental contexts provides an alternative perspective toward identity development models that largely purport linear models of development with clearly marked stages and a definitive end point.

With regard to direct practice, identity-based discussions have shown to be effective in addressing counseling concerns of Asian American college students (Chen, Johnson, & Takesue, 2007). In their study of Duke

University and Brown University Asian American students, using culturally relevant counseling approaches assisted greatly in their addressing mental health concerns and communal support (Chen et al. 2007). Particularly of note within Chen et al.'s article is the subjects' preference of such counseling spaces over those of Asian American student organizations, which according to the subjects were too political in nature to discuss the issues relevant to them. These varied interests within the campus community and the desired means by which to pursue them should also alert practitioners to develop a multifaceted approach to student services which addresses the varying degrees of learning styles and identity development which characterize the student body as a whole.

Family and Intergenerational Concerns

In addition to their concerns on campus, as a population whose families predominantly consist of first-generation immigrants and their 1.5- or second-generation children, family influence and intergenerational concerns continue to play a significant role in the lives of Asian American college students. Intergenerational conflict has often been discussed within the context of the interactions that Asian American students have with their families and communities, who often play a supplemental role in raising children and thus create an additional layer of filial piety and obligation beyond the traditional, immediate family. A number of researchers have approached these concerns by comparing Asian Americans to other ethnic or racial groups. In a study of three Asian American ethnic groups (East Asian American, Southeast Asian American, Filipino American/Pacific Islander) and European American college students, all of the Asian American ethnic groups indicated a lower level of educational satisfaction and college adjustment (Chang, Heckhausen, Greenberger, & Chen, 2009). Chang et al. explain that their educational satisfaction and college adjustment may be linked to their perceived lower levels of parental support, accommodation, and parental directing. Furthermore, since Asian American college students have reported the highest levels of family conflict compared to their Hispanic and European counterparts (Lee & Liu, 2001), this topic becomes a great concern within the higher education context, wherein these students, as young adults, attempt to balance their newfound independence with their ongoing familial obligations. Within Asian American and immigrant families, these conflicts often occur over such issues as shared custodial care of dependent family members, financial dependence, campus/career choice, and academic achievement/persistence. The mechanisms by which Asian American students cope with intergenerational family conflict have indicated that although students' use of both social support and problem solving strategies were often used, social support appeared to be the most effective (Lee, Su, & Yoshida, 2005). More specifically, Su, Lee, and Vang (2005) found that Hmong American college students having a strong social support network of co-ethnic students rather than using traditional problem-solving methods are more effective in relieving family conflict. Louie (2001) studied the influence that socioeconomic class has on Chinese American students and their family support. She found that middle class parents relied on private schooling and direct involvement in their children's education whereas working class Chinese parents used their social connections to help in their children's education.

Along similar lines, other researchers linked parent–child conflict with cultural values. In their study of Korean American college students, Ahn, Kim, and Park (2008) found that the perceived parent–child conflict tended to be intensified if there is a perception of a wide gap between adhered traditional values (e.g., dating and marriage). In addition, Einarson and Clarkberg (2010) contend that the more students showed flexibility in understanding the differences with the parents, then the less likely they would encounter parent–child conflicts that involved traditional values. Maramba (2013a) found that Filipino American college students invest a considerable amount of time negotiating their family and education environments. For example, Filipino Americans often considered their Filipino American identity versus their parents' immigrant Filipino identity, their values, and the current and potential conflicts that arise from these interactions. Moreover, Filipino American college students' navigation of their home and educational environments is often a difficult and consistently challenging negotiation process (Maramba, 2008a, 2013a). Their immigrant Filipino parents often played a significant role in their decision making as a college student (Maramba, 2008a, 2013a).

Similarly, Gim Chung (2001) explains that Asian American women experience more conflict over relationships than men but Asian American students who were of later generations reported lower levels of intergenerational conflict, perhaps due to decreased cultural dissonance between successive generations of American-born families. Self-blame also played a critical role in students reporting higher levels of distress when they blame themselves rather than their parents for intergenerational conflict. The immense strain that occurs when Asian American students feel torn between two seemingly irreconcilable cultures and communities can have irreparable effects on their mental health, leaving students permanently marginalized between two worlds, unable to decide which path is the "correct" one to follow. Thus, the mental health of Asian American students is a crucial and inherent aspect of the collegiate experience that must be addressed in order to effectively serve this population.

Mental Health

Given the importance of the overall mental health of college students, a few studies have focused on the mental health of Asian Americans. Though mental health issues concern all students, Asian Americans students' mental health seeking behaviors continue to be of serious concern (Huang, 2012; Hwang & Goto, 2009; Takemoto & Hayashino, 2012). Among the major factors that affect these issues include the effective and low utilization and stigma of mental health or counseling services (Chen, Sullivan, Lu, & Shibusawa, 2003; Kearney, Draper, & Baron, 2005; Miville & Constantine, 2007), ongoing assumptions from student services that Asian Americans do not need such services (Suzuki, 2002), multicultural competence of counselors (Wang & Kim, 2010), and the perceptions that Asian American students themselves have about counseling services on campus (Kearney et al., 2005; Mallinckrodt, Shigeoka, & Suzuki, 2005). Moreover, perceived racial discrimination and racial microaggressions (Sue, Bucceri, Lin, Nadal, & Torino, 2007), and a negative college climate continue to play an adverse role in their overall college experience and cause undue stress for AAPI students (Hwang

& Goto, 2009; Wei, Ku, & Liao, 2011). In other words, students are highly unlikely to turn to the university to solve their problems if they view that same university to be a significant cause of their stress.

Issues surrounding depression and suicidal behavior of Asian American students are brought to attention by a number of studies (Cress & Ikeda, 2003; Han & Lee, 2011; Kisch, Leino, & Silverman, 2005; Wong, Brownson, & Schwing, 2011). Depression among college students often has been connected to the campus climate (Cress & Ikeda, 2003). Furthermore, campus climate in and of itself is not a universal phenomenon but dependent on each students' educational context and perceived interactions with the campus on an interpersonal and institutional level. According to Cress and Ikeda (2003), Asian Americans are more likely to report feelings of depression and perceive their college climate as negative. In addition, college men in the study reported higher levels of depression than women. These findings continue to speak toward the need to evaluate Asian American students along multiple identities in order to truly understand their perspectives on their collegiate experience.

High collective esteem was also positively related to campus climate and the number of peers of the same racial/ethnic group on campus (Kim & Lee, 2011). On that note, high collective self-esteem in one's membership was more prevalent in Asian Americans of later generations (Kim & Lee, 2011). However, it is often hard to consider this factor in serving mental health concerns of Asian Americans given the prevalent stereotype of Asian Americans as perpetual foreigners. While a study on Hmong college students states that despite the difficulties of acculturation both in and out of the classroom, the majority of the participants in the study cited overall optimism that their life would improve (S. C. Lee, 2007). Studies on depression among Vietnamese college students have shown to establish a correlation with racial discrimination and poor mental health (Han & Lee, 2011). Other associated factors for Vietnamese students include not having successful peer networks as well as intergenerational conflict with their parents and perceived racial discrimination (Han & Lee, 2011). Along similar lines, Wong et al. (2011) studied Asian American students and suicidal ideation. Among the students who contemplated suicide, common factors and events included family, academic, financial, and social problems. It was also posited that among a number of factors associated with suicidal ideation, there was a positive correlation with involvement in a student organization. This correlation seems to counter other research, which has concluded that peer networks and student organizations are beneficial in mediating campus adjustment and social concerns of Asian American students. However, the authors speculated that students may be more exposed to racism and injustice issues as they become more exposed to other students with different racial backgrounds, thus contributing to feelings of helplessness, depression, and suicidal ideation due to being unable to combat the hostile structural forces surrounding them. Another possible interpretation was that students who seek out social circles are already skewed toward poor self-esteem and mental health.

Other studies have focused on the links between mental and physical health concerns of Asian Americans, which include episodic drinking (Iwamoto, Corbin, & Fromme, 2010), smoking behaviors (Otsuki, 2009), and HIV risks and substance abuse (So, Wong, & DeLeon, 2005; Yi & Daniel, 2001). Collectively, this research concludes that Asian American students, in search of meaningful campus experiences and relationships, are much more likely to compromise their health by engaging in high-risk behavior that would garner social acceptance. In the case of episodic drinking, the results found that drinking was related to lower parent involvement. While on average, the levels of heavy episodic drinking among Asian Americans were lower than those of other races, those Asian Americans who reported the highest levels of drinking compared with high-risk groups of all other races (Iwamoto et al., 2010). In a study conducted by Otsuki (2009), smoking was found to serve as a "social lubricant" for Asian Americans and that social aspects of smoking may be related to their overall desire to find a comfortable space within campus. With regard to risk factors for HIV and drug/alcohol use, Asian Americans have shown to have very low knowledge about HIV but also found that time in college had a stronger correlation to higher risk behavior in these activities than merely time spent acculturating to the United States (So et al., 2005). Each of these cases illustrates the strong tendencies of Asian Americans to compromise various aspects of their physical health in both the short and long terms in attempts to make meaningful connections and experiences within the college environment, the significance of which we will discuss further in the following section regarding extracurricular leadership and involvement.

Leadership and Involvement

The existing literature on the involvement of Asian American students on college campuses involves discussion of leadership development and engagement in student organizations and campus-wide student government. When considering the leadership of Asian Americans, researchers explained that cultural factors and the impact of racism facilitate a central part in their student leadership development (Liang, Lee, & Ting, 2002). Student leadership development programs that focus and utilize values in leadership and culture allow Asian Americans to more likely perceive themselves as leaders and develop a larger sociopolitical consciousness (Liang et al., 2002). However, conversely, the work of Balón (2003, 2005) and Balón and Shek (2013) reinforced the issue that although Asian Americans believe in the importance of cultural awareness in leadership, Asian Americans are less likely to see themselves as leaders compared to their African American and White counterparts. They also feel less confident about being able to make a difference in the community. So while they hope to achieve and attain culturally relevant experiences, they are less confident in their abilities (whether on an individual or structural level) to actually facilitate these experiences for themselves and others.

On the whole, involvement in student organizations has shown to be a salient interest in improving the experience of Asian American undergraduates. Their involvement in these organizations and diversity-related activities has resulted in a greater understanding of Asian American issues (Inkelas, 2004). Similarly, involvement in ethnic organizations aided in the cultural adjustment to the college campus and further cultural validation in predominantly White institutions (Museus, 2008). Studies have also discussed more specific activity within particular subsets of student organizations such as Greek letter organizations and religious organizations. These organizations, not unlike generalized racial/ethnic cultural organizations, are also founded upon similar principles of giving underrepresented students a voice within an arena where it has often been excluded and discarded (Gonzalez, 2012; Park 2008). However, Gonzalez explained that although Asian American Greek letter organizations have existed almost as long as other Greek letter minority organizations and "mainstream" racial/ethnic organizations, they have not been given appropriate attention and support by college campuses, as their organizational mission statements often do not completely align with either the Greek system or Asian American cultural organizations as a whole. Along ethnic and religious identities, Park's research on Korean American students' decisions between joining a homogenous and racially diverse campus religious group provided a deeper understanding of how religion and ethnicity influence comfort zones and personal growth (Park, 2011). Explorations of the ways in which religion, a seemingly race-neutral cultural space, has become increasingly racialized on college campuses (Abelmann, 2009) speak to the continued segregation, which occurs in higher education at all levels. Overall, student engagement with racial- and ethnic-specific campus organizations has encouraged collective activity among the Asian American and Pacific Islander racial group, the effects of which are largely positive thus far but also largely unexplored as a whole (Rhoads, Lee, & Yamada, 2002). Moving forward, as these organizations grow larger and more rooted within the history of particular campuses, more research must be done to evaluate their qualitative impact on college access, retention, and recruitment in a similar fashion to other mainstream extracurricular activities that are seen as an inevitable part of the college experience such as sports and Greek life.

College Choice

College and career choices have shown to be important factors in students' curricular and extracurricular decision-making processes within their institutions of higher education (Dundes, Cho, & Kwak, 2009; Kim, 2004; Kim & Gasman, 2011; Tang, 2002). Factors that play a role in college choice are not simply academic prestige of the institution but also its location, cost, and applicant's fit with the individual campus culture. Additionally, for AAPI college students, there is also a high correlation between having immigrant parents and having higher levels of family interdependence, which may suggest that

TABLE 2
Distribution of Selected Institutional Characteristics by Ethnicity

	Percentage Among				
	Chinese Americans	Filipino Americans	Japanese Americans	Korean Americans	Southeast Asians
Low selectivity	65.4	81.5	74	62	75.4
High selectivity	34.6	18.5	26	38.1	24.6
Four-year public college	26.7	43.6	30.5	27.3	32
Four-year private college	14.8	15.9	29.8	19	15.9
Four-year public university	35.8	27.8	21.4	36.5	38.4
Four-year private university	22.7	12.7	18.3	17.2	13.7

Note: Weighted *N* = 66,561. Percentage sign (%) has been eliminated.
Source: Teranishi, R. T. (2010). "Analysis of data from the Cooperative Institutional Research Program" (CIRP, 2010). *Asians in the Ivory Tower* (p. 115). New York, NY: Teachers College Press. Adapted with permission.

family obligations can influence their academic pursuits (Tseng, 2004). As Table 2 illustrates, these factors actually result in a far more varied distribution of Asian American students along the higher education pipeline than the model minority stereotype or the meritocratic ideal of the best and the brightest attending the most elite schools might suggest. Contrary to the model minority myth of Asian American academic success at elite institutions, statistics show that a majority of Asian Americans are actually attending low selectivity institutions rather than highly selective ones, and there are extremely varied enrollment patterns among institutional types between Asian American ethnicities. Most notably, there is an achievement gap within the Asian American category between Southeast Asians and Filipino Americans versus East Asian ethnicities.

Our review of extant literature regarding college choice and matriculation illustrates that these enrollment disparities are not simply illustrative of rational decisions based on one's objective college-going qualifications. In a study conducted of predominantly Chinese and Taiwanese Americans, findings suggest that most students relied on family and peer networks as primary influences in their college choice. Also important in this examination is that college in and of itself was not a choice but part of a linear trajectory (Kim & Gasman, 2011). Furthermore, in order to analyze the intersections of race and socioeconomic class, Kim (2004) examined the effect of financial aid on college choice for students of color. While all Asian American, African American, and Latino students were less likely to attend their first-choice college compared to their White counterparts, being granted any type of financial aid was indeed a significant factor in college choice for Asian Americans. An important finding of this study suggested that Asian American students who attended their first-choice institution are willing to attend their first-choice college regardless of the financial burden. Likewise, among the findings of a 2007 report based on Asian/Asian American first-time, full-time college students (Chang et al., 2007) the ability to finance a college education played an important role in applying to college and the college choice process. Within communities of color, particularly among immigrant families which predominate the Asian American communities, access to financial aid is not just a quantitative evaluation of one's family income but also widely reflective of a prospective student and her/his family's cultural capital. That is, their ability to access and understand (both linguistically and culturally) resources such as the Free Application for Federal Student Aid (FAFSA), private loans, scholarships, or even pooling together money from family and community in order to fund a college education.

In a study that examined both college and career choice of East Asian students in the United States, findings indicated that Asian parents were more likely to emphasize prestige of a college over happiness in college and career selection for their children (Dundes et al., 2009). Parental influence and students' career choice appeared to play a prominent role for Asian American and Chinese groups (Tang, 2002). More specifically, they were more likely to choose "investigative" occupations versus their White counterparts who were more likely to choose "social" occupations. Furthermore, Asian Americans and Chinese students were more likely to compromise with their parents regarding their career choices whereas White students insisted on their autonomy (Tang, 2002). Along similar lines, Lowe (2005) found that career counselors who used collectivist approaches were rated higher by Asian American students. Techniques such as integrating the exploration of family involvement in career decisions and other external obligations proved to be effective because they provided students with more realistic options that considered their cultural context. Overall, the literature on college choice and career choice of Asian Americans, although still lacking, provides information that is useful for implementing strategies for better serving this population.

Community College

Disaggregating data on AAPIs is also important with regard to examining Asian Americans within different institutional types (i.e., four-year institutions versus two-year institutions, levels of selectivity between institutions, etc.). The largest sector of AAPIs attending postsecondary institutions in 2005 was located in community colleges (47.3%; see Figure 8). Additionally, between the years 1990 and 2000, the AAPI community college going population increased 73.3% compared to only a 42.2% increase at four-year institutions (CARE, 2011). As the Figure 8 shows, Asian American and Pacific Islander college students are an extremely varied group between two- and four-year colleges. The social, economic, cultural, and academic contexts that preclude enrollment at either type of institution leave students vulnerable to various risk factors that are associated with dropping out, stopping out, and being pushed out of higher education. These risk factors include but are not limited to being the first member of one's family to attend college, caring for dependent family members (whether physically, emotionally, and/or financially), working full-time, being enrolled part-time, paying for college with borrowed money, or not being a native English speaker. Surveys of Asian American students at two- and four-year institutions illustrate that risk factors are more prevalent among the two-year institution student population. Whereas most students in four-year institutions tend to predominantly navigate zero, one, or two risk factors that may obstruct their degree attainment, Asian American students at two-year colleges tend to be just the opposite— dealing with one, two, and even more risk factors. When we then consider that a majority of Asian American college students are concentrated in two-year institutions, the stereotypes of academic excellence among this

FIGURE 8
Number of Risk Factors for Asian American and Pacific Islander Students by Institutional Type (2003–2004)

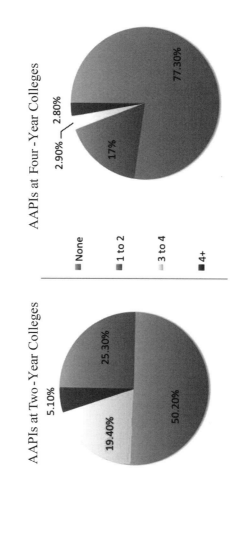

AAPIs at Two-Year Colleges

AAPIs at Four-Year Colleges

None
1 to 2
3 to 4
4+

Source: U.S. Department of Education, BPS Longitudinal Study, First Follow-Up. (2011). From "The Relevance of Asian American and Pacific Islanders in the College Completion Agenda" (p. 10). *The National Commission on Asian American and Pacific Islanders Research in Education.* Adapted with permission.

student population are seriously called into question. Therefore, the push for disaggregated research on Asian American students should not merely emphasize their ethnicity, nationality, and/or language proficiency, but also just as importantly their academic status and potential links to risk factors which may obstruct retention.

Outside of four-year institutions, research on AAPIs in community college continues to be limited, despite the fact that the largest sectors of AAPI college students are located in community colleges. Specifically, AAPI subgroups as Loatians, Cambodians, Vietnamese and Hmong are more likely to enroll in community colleges (Teranishi, 2010). Despite the dearth of data, the available studies that are focused on community college have been indeed helpful in depicting Asian American students' needs and capabilities both in and out of the classroom. In a similar fashion to their counterparts at universities, Asian American community college students also find difficulties in adjusting to campus climate. Asian American groups at the community college level were found to have the lowest levels of faculty interaction out of all racial groups. AAPI students also reported feeling strongly that "things are harder because of their race or ethnicity" (Chang, 2005, p. 789). Moreover, in one study of Japanese, Chinese, Filipino, and Native Hawaiian and White community college students, Orsuwan (2011) explained that residual effects of the stratified hierarchy within the context of Hawaii had a negative influence on the educational experiences of the participants in the study, particularly for the Native Hawaiian students and Filipinos who were also mistakenly racialized as such. These historical contexts of race relations and power can also be applied throughout the United States, where Asian Americans have been victims of institutional discrimination throughout history, the effects of which are still evident in many educational settings. In a similar study, Orsuwan and Cole (2007) explored the links between educational satisfaction and ethnicity. Chinese Americans with college educated parents and Native Hawaiian students with low parental education were less satisfied with their educational experience. Researchers also found that there was a correlation between the larger demographic with overall higher satisfaction, as was the case for Filipino American community college students. With regard to distinct challenges between disaggregated APA ethnic groups, Wang, Chang, and Lew

(2009) found that only 20% spoke English as their first language and more than half attended school in another country. Also important in this study is that Chinese, Vietnamese, and Pacific Islander students were least likely to have parents who are college graduates. When these experiences of Asian American students within two- and four-year institutions are evaluated in tandem, researchers are able to see a more holistic picture of the social, cultural, political, and economic contexts which influence Asian American matriculation into higher education long before the seemingly objective and meritocratic variables of academics come into play. Therefore, we are now seeing an emergence of institutional resources and policies, which seek to address these conditions in order to directly benefit these underserved student populations.

The Emergence of Asian American and Native American Pacific Islander–Serving Institutions (AANAPISIs)

AANAPISIs are the most recently designated Minority Serving Institutions (MSIs), along with Historically Black Colleges and Universities (HBCUs), Tribal Colleges and Universities (TCUs), and Hispanic Serving Institutions (HSIs). The evolution of AANAPISIs occurred in increments (Park & Teranishi, 2008) and came with a number of challenges. First, advocates in the field of educational research and policy needed to combat the ongoing misperception of AAPIs as having little to no concerns in education and their assumed high academic achievement. Second, the existing aggregated data on AAPIs made it challenging to understand the concerns of underserved AAPI subgroups (Teranishi et al., 2012). In light of these increasing concerns and awareness of the lack of educational, community, and social service needs of the growing APA student populations, a 2001 report by the White House Initiative on Asian Americans and Pacific Islanders (WHIAPPI) recommended federal designation for Asian Americans and Pacific Islanders (Park & Teranishi, 2008). The pivotal moment came in May 2002 when Congressman Robert Underwood (D-Guam) formally proposed an amendment to the Higher

Education Act of 1965 (U.S. Congress, H.R. 4825) recommending authorization to provide funding for colleges and universities that served Asian Americans and Pacific Islanders (Park & Teranishi, 2008). In reappraising the original mission, H.R. 4825 was reintroduced in the House of Representatives and eventually in the Senate. Congressman David Wu (D-OR) first reintroduced it in 2003 and in 2005 it became H.R. 2616 as a Senate companion bill S. 2160 by Senators Barbara Boxer (D-CA) and Daniel Akaka (D-HI) which came to be known the Asian American and Pacific Islander Serving Institutions Act (Park & Teranishi, 2008).

The official designation of the AANAPISI federal program was instituted in 2007 as part of the College Cost Reduction and Access Act of 2007 (CARE, 2010). One of the major aims of the AANAPISI program aimed to provide grants to institutions that already serve a large number of AAPI students. About two thirds of the AAPI undergraduate enrollment in 2009 were concentrated in only 200 institutions, primarily in California, Hawaii, Illinois, New York, Massachusetts, Maryland, Texas, Washington, and the unincorporated territory of Guam (CARE, 2011). The AANAPISI grant program requires that institutions must first apply to be designated as an AANAPISI and would then be allowed to apply for AANAPISI grant funding for their institution. In order for a designated institution to be considered an AANAPISI and eligible to apply for grant funding, the higher education institution must be public or private nonprofit, accredited and degree granting, and must have at least 10% of AAPI students and at least 50% of the degree-seeking students receiving federal financial aid (U.S. Department of Education, 2010). In addition, an institution must also hold a minimum threshold of low-income students, and lower than average cost expenditure per student to compete for an AANAPISI grant (CARE, 2010, 2011; Laanan & Starobin, 2004; Teranishi et al., 2012).

As of 2011, there are 148 institutions that meet the criteria of being designated as an AANAPISI, and this number is projected to increase to 160 in 2013. However, to date, there are a total of only 52 higher education institutions officially designated as an AANAPISI (CARE, 2011) and only 25 received funding through the grant competition (U.S. Department of Education, 2013; Table 3). Notably, the majority of the 25 funded AANAPISIs

TABLE 3
List of Asian American and Native American Pacific Islander–Serving Institutions (AANAPISIs) Program Grantees (2008–2013)

Institution	State	Year Awarded
City College of San Francisco	CA	2008
Seattle Community College	WA	2008
University of Maryland, College Park	MD	2008
University of Hawaii at Hilo	HI	2008, 2011
Foothill-De Anza Community College District	CA	2008, 2011
Guam Community College	GU	2008
Queens College/CUNY	NY	2009
Santa Monica College	CA	2009
Guam Community College	GU	2009
University of Massachusetts, Boston	MA	2010
Mission Community College	CA	2010
University of Illinois, Chicago	IL	2010, 2011
Peralta Community College	CA	2010
Coast Community College	CA	2010
Richland College	TX	2010
San Francisco Community College District	CA	2010
University of Guam	GU	2010
American Samoa Community College	AS	2011
Mt. San Antonio College	CA	2011
Mission College	CA	2011
San Jose State Foundation	CA	2011
California State University, Sacramento	CA	2011
California State University, East Bay	CA	2011
Palau Community College	PW	2011
South Seattle Community College	WA	2011

Source: Adapted from http://www2.ed.gov/programs/aanapi/awards.html. Please note that no new awards were granted for 2012 and 2013.

are public two-year colleges. This is important because a disproportionate number of AAPI students are concentrated in two-year institutions (47.3%) and their enrollment in community colleges is projected to increase (CARE, 2011). Though AAPIs make up less than 5% of the national population, they make up 7% of all community college students (CARE, 2011).

The relatively new designation of AANAPISIs creates a wealth of opportunities for growing research related to the students for whom it's designed to serve. In gathering aspects of the limited qualitative data already collected, research indicates that AAPI students from specific ethnic groups who enter these institutions are first-generation college students, come from underserved (underresourced) high schools, and are underprepared for college-level work due to socioeconomic status (Palmer, Maramba, Gasman, & Lloyd, 2013). For example, the educational attainment of the AAPI population is bimodal. More than four out of five Chinese, Japanese, Koreans, Asian Indian, and Pakistani students earned at least a bachelor's degree. However, the numbers of Southeast Asians who attended but did not earn a degree are highly disproportionate (42.9% Cambodian; 47.5% Hmong; 46.5% Laotian; and 33.7% Vietnamese) compared to their AAPI counterparts (e.g., 8.2% Asian Indian; 12.5% Chinese; and 12.7% Pakistani; CARE, 2011). With regard to AAPI community college students, they have a higher likelihood, compared to other racial and ethnic groups, to have a difficulty in financing their education. This is the case because AAPI community college students have higher financial need (45.5% have more than $2,000 in need, and 10.6% are more than $8,900 in need) and are less likely to seek federal financial aid compared to other racial/ethnic groups (CARE, 2010). As we have mentioned previously in this chapter, difficulty in financing a college education is not simply an objective evaluation of one's income, but also an evaluation of one's ability to access and understand the complex and nuanced sources of financial assistance available to college students.

Upon a closer examination of some of the contextual factors affecting AAPI students, the 2010 National Commission on Asian American and Pacific Islander Research in Education (CARE) report provided a number of examples that reflect the complexity of the AAPI population and thus highlighted the need for institutions which address the specific needs of these students. For example, the University of Hawaii at Hilo had an average poverty rate for Pacific Islanders that was 20.1%, nearly twice the national average of 12.4%. Similarly, South Seattle Community College, where a large number of Southeast Asian Americans and immigrants reside, 57.8% of Asian Americans and 70.8% of Pacific Islanders attained a high school diploma or less (CARE, 2010). In terms of academic preparation and readiness, many arrive on campuses underprepared. At De Anza College, most of the AAPI students are not prepared for college-level work and they account for more than half of all students enrolled in remedial English and other basic skills classes. More than 80% of the students enrolled at Guam Community College were eligible for financial aid and 58% of the students were nontraditionally aged students (18–22 years of age constituting the traditional age; CARE, 2010). Clearly, the significance of the AANAPISIs goes hand in hand with evidence for the range and diversity within the Asian American student body and indicates relevant services that they need upon matriculation. While the aims of AANAPISIs are to focus on student services, curriculum and academic programs, and resources and research, the challenges that students continue to face will require critical attention (Table 4; CARE, 2011). Although the goals of AANAPISI program are the same with regard to effectively addressing the needs of their AAPI students, each institution used their funding in utilizing different approaches to address their unique institutional contexts. Table 4 presents examples of the various projects and programs that AANAPISIs implemented at their respective institutions. As indicated, the desired outcomes are likely common goals that funded AANAPISIs' share; however, various types of programs with regard to implementing student services, curricular, academic, and resource development may differ depending on the institutions' approach in addressing the students' needs. Through providing student services, improving curricular development, and resource and research development, AANAPISIs have high potential for effectively addressing the issues that concern the AAPI population.

Throughout this chapter, we have established that the Asian American student experience goes far beyond statistical representation in admissions but is also heavily influenced by what happens before and during students' time on campus. Asian American experiences traverse boundaries of cultures, communities, and countries, creating far more diverse and unique perspectives on the cost and value of higher education than can be summarily unified under the banner of "Asian American." Therefore, we conclude the monograph with practical implications for research, programming, and administration, which can hopefully serve as a more holistic blueprint to not only serve Asian American students but also allow educational professionals to better understand and serve all underrepresented and marginalized student populations.

TABLE 4
Descriptive Data on AANAPISI Programs and Services

Type of Programming	Examples of AANAPISI Projects	Desired Outcomes
Student services	Academic achievement programs	Increase grades of underperforming minority students in core courses, increase success in gatekeeper courses.
	Freshman transition/bridge programs	Increase college access and persistence in the first year of college.
	College transfer programs	Improve the transition, progression, transfer, and graduation rates.
	Educational engagement initiatives	Connect students to community, enhance student support services, engage students on campus.
Curricular and academic program development	English language learner program improvement	
	Develop a more collaborative curriculum	
	Asian American and Pacific Islander studies programs	Create/enhance curriculum that introduces knowledge about AAPI communities.
	AAPI student leadership programs	Improve academic and leadership skills, critical and analytic thought, high-level organization, and public speaking skills.
	Faculty and staff development workshops	Educate faculty and staff to better understand the complexities of the AAPI student population.
Resource and research development	Learning resource centers	Create accessible space for student use.
	Initiatives to improve collection and analysis of data on AAPI students	Improve systems of data collection on AAPI students.

Source: CARE. (2011). "Descriptive Data on AANAPISI Programs and Services." *The National Commission on Asian American and Pacific Islanders Research in Education.* Adapted with permission.

Conclusions and Recommendations

I N THE FIRST PART OF THIS VOLUME we began with a discussion of the evolution of the model minority myth, a stereotype that continues to plague the narrative on Asian Americans. Within this first chapter, we incorporated analytical discussions and approaches by critical race theorists and AsianCrit scholars who have challenged dominant discourses and transformed our discussion of the AAPI population. In the second chapter, we presented a brief history of Asian Americans in higher education, which includes their institutionalized segregation in public schools and their student activism on college campuses. Moreover, we also incorporated the profound influence of Asian Americans' little-known engagement with and contributions to the Civil Rights Movement. In the third chapter, we discussed how the presence of Asian Americans problematizes the ongoing Affirmative Action admissions debate. Included in this chapter are the effects of the past and present court cases that impacted how Asian Americans are situated in present-day affirmative action deliberations. The fourth chapter covered extant literature on the social and academic experiences of Asian Americans on college campuses. Also discussed are factors and issues that affect their overall developmental experiences in postsecondary institutions. The following is a discussion of our recommendations for future research, policy, and practice based on our examination of the AAPI literature.

Recommendations for Future Research: Purposeful Disaggregation of Data

It is clear from the literature that the AAPI population is vastly diverse, composed of 48 ethnic groups (CARE, 2011). AAPIs differ largely with regard to socioeconomic status, immigration status and history, language, culture, and religion. Not only is the demography of AAPIs rapidly changing, it is also a fast-growing population that is predicted to reach 40 million in the United States by the year 2050 (CARE, 2011). Thus, when studying the AAPI student population, it is not wise to approach AAPI students as a monolithic group. In order to create a more authentic picture of the AAPI population, data on AAPIs must be intentionally disaggregated by ethnic subgroups and critically analyzed. Equally important is conducting further research using varied qualitative and quantitative methodologies to gain a wider, clearer, and critical understanding of AAPIs. Additionally, it is also clear that more empirical studies that involve specific AAPI populations (e.g., Pacific Islanders, Native Hawaiian, Southeast Asian Americans, Filipino Americans, Desi, and Burmese) and intersectionalities as gender, class, and immigration status will provide a better understanding of the complexity of the AAPI category.

While it is important to understand the historical context of the "model minority" as being rooted in race prejudice, it is also important to acknowledge its negative effects and how it continues to mask the current realities of AAPI ethnic groups. These negative outcomes have manifested in a variety of ways. For example, very little is known about the extent of AAPI participation in STEM (science, technology, engineering, and math) fields. In a comprehensive review of STEM participation by Museus, Palmer, Davis, and Maramba (2011), the study of AAPIs is limited. A number of resources state that the study of Asian Americans in STEM is severely limited by a number of factors (e.g., CARE, 2011; Maramba, 2013b; Museus et al., 2011; Teranishi et al., 2012). First, aggregated statistical data on the math performance, SAT math scores, and STEM degree aspirants who completed a STEM degree appear to show that Asian Americans are successful. Therefore, the predominant conclusion is that they are in need of little attention. However, disaggregated data indicate that specific Asian ethnic groups (e.g., Southeast

Asian Americans and Pacific Islanders) are indeed underrepresented in STEM fields (CARE, 2010). Disaggregated data and more specific data on particular Asian American ethnic groups in STEM, in addition to gendered experiences (George-Jackson, 2011), need to be further studied in this area. In their study of Asian Americans in STEM, Teranishi et al. (2012) explained that there is indeed a concern regarding the low retention and success of particular AAPI ethnic groups in STEM majors. They concluded that it is vital to have support systems within the university that both recognize this issue and are committed to making a positive impact. The lack of critical disaggregation of data has also created perhaps yet another challenge to understanding the issues surrounding STEM and AAPI students. For example, federal organizations and funding agencies such as the National Science Foundation (NSF) state that AAPIs are not considered an underrepresented group and therefore excludes them from funding opportunities (Teranishi et al., 2012). This is all the more troubling when institutions of higher education use NSF's definitions to award campus fellowships and scholarships to underrepresented minority groups.

Multiracial AAPIs

In addition to gathering more purposeful, disaggregated data on AAPI students, there exists a growing need to pay attention to multiracial Asian American students. Some of the research on multiracial or biracial AAPI students on college campuses indicates that simplistic notions of ethnic identities (as identifying with either/or ethnic/racial group) become complicated and nuanced (Andrews & Chun, 2007). Students' situational contexts, how they feel in terms of identifying with particular racial categories, and their reasons for identity shifting require further qualitative research. In considering the out-marriage rates among AAPI populations, how students redefine the definition of "Asian American" in the future will be of particular import. Gauging multiracial AAPI students' notions of racial formation can add important discussions on the larger discourse surrounding race. Other scholars would argue that Asian Americans have always existed in multidimensional ways, in relation to ethnic identity, and that current research needs to reflect such diversity (Espiritu, 2001).

Research Beyond the Model Minority

This monograph also covered recent historical developments that gave way to modern conceptions of how Asian Americans began to be perceived as the model minority. While extant research examines the development of the stereotype and its manifestations across the K–16 pipeline (Hartlep, 2013), more critical studies that work to decenter Asian Americans as the model minorities, as well as providing multiracial frameworks for unraveling that concept, are needed. Questioning the basis of Asian American academic achievement through critical, historical, and qualitative studies will yield rich data. In that light, increased focus coming from the humanistic and social science disciplines that analyze the intersectionalities of race, class, and sexual orientation to the study of Asian Americans in education would offer fresh perspectives and create linkages with research in the fields of ethnic studies and gender and women studies (Coloma, 2006; Lei, 2003).

Another way to complicate the model minority concept can come through increased research on AAPI populations in the community college sector. Whereas the majority of AAPI students attend community colleges, there still exists a dearth of knowledge about the particularities of students in those institutions. While the attention to AAPIs is important, more research from critical quantitative and qualitative methodologies with an AsianCrit focus will be helpful.

Implications for Policy

Higher education administrators who influence and develop campus policies have a unique opportunity to create meaningful changes that reflect the heterogeneity of AAPI populations. Grounded in solid, disaggregated empirical and qualitative evidence, policymakers can consider the myriad ways that AAPI students experience campus life.

On a policy level, a number of reasons can be considered. First, without critically collected data on AAPIs, the affirmative action debate will continue to unfairly use AAPIs as a wedge between other populations of color as well as the White population. With disaggregated data that show the educational disparities among AAPI ethnic groups, policy makers will have more accurate data to be able to make more informed decisions thus creating more effective and equitable policy. Yet another point to consider is that how we have come to think about the concept of affirmative action in higher education is really a function of negative action. These two very distinct ideas require further clarification and understanding. This is evident in the case of the AAPI population and can be used as an opportunity for critically transforming the discourse on affirmative action. Foregrounding how AAPIs experience higher education in racialized ways becomes an important feature in devising culturally relevant policies that take into account the inclusive experiences of all AAPI students.

For example, considering particular institutional contexts as it affects Asian American ethnic groups can begin to address notable gaps in policies and services. The creation of a Hmong American studies focus, the first of its kind in the nation, at the University of Wisconsin-Madison (UW-Madison), and the hiring of a tenure-track faculty member in that field, signals important shifts in linking research, policy, and practice. UW-Madison's recognition of the growing student population and the need for an area of academic study focused on Hmong Americans is a step in the right direction. In addition, with the recent emergence of AANAPISIs (Asian American and Native American Pacific Islander–Serving Institutions) in higher education, future research in this area will be beneficial in addressing the disparities within the AAPI populations.

Implications for Practice

Our examination also has implications for practice. Our findings from the literature reflect a dire need for student affairs practitioners, staff, faculty, and administrators to improve their understanding of the AAPI population. This understanding can be facilitated in a number of ways. First, the presentation of and access to AAPI data, that is, disaggregated data is important for institutional research offices, which can then help assess how best to serve AAPI populations. Useful data and the critical interpretation of disaggregated data can be disseminated via consistent and ongoing staff development and training. Student affairs personnel involved in counseling, advising, and health services must be especially familiar with, if not thoroughly knowledgeable on the academic, social, and psychological adjustment of AAPIs to college.

Having institutions understand these gaps and disparities in access and achievement provides more effective support for Asian American students. Chew-Ogi and Ogi (2002) address the need for successful ways of working with Asian Americans. For example, student affairs professionals must engage in critical dialogue about creating a supportive environment for this population that includes the perspectives of students, staff, faculty, and administrators. Likewise, in their study of Asian American students' use of student affairs offices, Yang, Byers, Ahuna, and Castro (2002) found that students who valued their familial heritage were also more likely to visit the university office designated to provide services to Asian American students. They also discuss the important role that student affairs offices can play in providing a welcoming campus environment and facilitating the effective use of their services by Asian Americans. Similarly, Liang and Sedlacek (2003) found that White student services practitioners subconsciously reinforced many stereotypes of Asian Americans as passive and timid. The researchers suggested that student affairs staff be provided with more effective training that explores their own attitudes toward Asian American students in order to better initiate their services. Overall, understanding the disparities in how Asian American students do or do not utilize campus services and how student affairs practitioners and university administrators address these issues will influence AAPIs' college experiences. It requires a thorough understanding and delivery of services that reflect *culturally sensitive and responsive practices.*

As revealed in the literature, support networks are an important component to the success of AAPIs. These support networks can involve areas such as residential life, student activities, and orientation in order to facilitate a more inclusive and inviting college environment. On the faculty level, it is equally important for faculty to understand the diversity of the AAPI population, and hiring faculty sensitive to AAPI issues (including AAPI faculty at all ranks). This knowledge can aid faculty in their understanding of diversity within their classroom and influence their pedagogical practices and dynamics in their classes. By realizing the needs of underserved AAPI ethnic groups, student affairs personnel can better provide resources to facilitate their successful adjustment to college.

Challenges Looming on the Horizon: Conflation of AAPI College Students and Asian International Undergraduates

In lieu of research which has accounted for the diverse ethnic, economic, and academic diversity within Asian America, little attention has been paid to the nationality of Asian Americans. Currently, institutions of higher education across the country are experiencing an influx of Asian students who are attending college in the United States on student visas. These students, classified as "international students," are often left out of the discourse on race, ethnicity, and diversity in the college environment. Therefore, the purpose of this conclusion section is to provide a snapshot of their current campus experiences and establish the many similarities and differences between Asian international students and their American-born counterparts.

According to the 2012 Open Doors Report from the Institute of International Education (IIE), international student enrollment in U.S. post-secondary institutions reached a record high of 764,495 in the 2011–2012 academic year. Asian countries comprise an overwhelming majority of this population with 546,634 students or 71%. More specifically, significant among these numbers is that the countries of China (194,029), India (100,270), South Korea (72,295), and Saudi Arabia (34,139) not only comprise the four largest nationalities of students, but among themselves account for the majority of international American students with 52% of the population. Furthermore, the number of students from China and Saudi Arabia displayed one-year population increases of 23.1% and 50.4%, respectively, well ahead of the international percentage increases of 8.4% from Asia and 5.7% worldwide.

While international students consist of less than 4% of the U.S. college student population, their population distribution is skewed toward a small number of states and institutions. Thus, in the same fashion as topics pertaining to their American-born counterparts, postsecondary educational policy, which seeks to target the Asian international student population, should not merely consider the quantitative but also the qualitative population demographics of these students. According to the IIE, two thirds of international students, or approximately 500,000, are concentrated within 200 colleges—5% of the total number of postsecondary institutions in the United States. One third of international students reside in California (102,789), New York (82,436), or Texas (61,511). Massachusetts, the state with the fourth largest international student population (41,258), also has the highest percentage of international students within their state's total college student body at 7.6%. The IIE's ranked list of colleges with the highest populations of international students indicates that 18 of the top 25 institutions are medium- or large-sized, research-based, public universities. Also of note is a list compiled by *U.S. News & World Report* (2012) that measures international student presence based on percentage of the overall student body. When the international student body is ranked in terms of proportion rather than raw number, this list illustrates that 22 of the top 25 schools are actually small or medium-sized private universities. These numbers reinforce the need to evaluate the Asian international presence from multiple perspectives in order to truly gauge its impact on the educational experiences of its students.

Between the IIE Open Doors Report, *U.S. News & World Report* rankings, and the self-authored population demographics of each individual university, international students are categorized among the student body in very inconsistent ways. Some institutions only create student profiles based on race/ethnicity, and do not differentiate within these categories based on nationality. In other cases, the opposite is true—student demographics regarding nationality are compiled, but these categories are not disaggregated by race/ethnicity and thus do not properly account for the diverse populations within these countries. Schools that release data on international students based on nationality offer the greatest opportunity for accurate statistical analysis of international students' contributions to the diversity of the campus climate due to the flexibility of the researcher to openly interpret disaggregated data based on the constantly evolving definitions of race and racial categories. However, disaggregated data regarding the nationality and ethnicity of international students is hardly ever accompanied by an equally disaggregated dataset of American students. Moving forward, a more comprehensive dataset, which integrates the race, ethnicity, and nationality of all students, would create a more accurate picture of the needs and capabilities of a student body that is becoming increasingly more diverse in each category.

Naturally, the increasing diversity in race, ethnicity, and nationality in colleges and universities carries over into the realms of academic and student services, where current research regarding the experiences of Asian international students illustrates that the most immediate needs of these students are acquiring the English language (in both academic and informal contexts) and dealing with feelings of homesickness (Poyrazli, Kavanaugh, Baker, & Al-Timmi, 2004; Tochkov, Levine, & Sanaka, 2010). While institutions must develop programming and curricula to address these immediate needs, they must also recognize that these needs are tied to larger sociocultural issues of becoming acculturated to campus climate, the pressure to succeed academically and economically, and the ability to develop networks with peers from both their home and host nations. Furthermore, it is imperative to recognize the power dynamics within the campus environment that prevents international students from proactively seeking and engaging in academic and student services and reconfigure outreach efforts accordingly. As with any other student demographic, then, academic and student services professionals should remember that they should not just treat the symptoms but also attack the root of the problem.

Large-scale surveys of international students have indicated that the primary concern among this population is English proficiency due to its correlation with academic self-esteem and self-efficacy. Conversely, a lack of English proficiency has been linked to higher levels of stress among international students (Kwon, 2009; Wilton & Constantine, 2003). Research on students and stress-related services has previously found that Asian American students are the least likely of all racial groups to seek professional counseling services due to cultural values, which emphasize self-reliance and stigmatize mental health services. The rate of use of counseling services falls even lower for Asian international students (Chang & Chang, 2004). While they hold many of the same cultural beliefs as their American counterparts who are typically no more than one generation removed from Asia themselves, international students become further alienated from counseling services due to the language barrier as well as the belief that, as visitors to this country, they are not entitled to student services and resources (Major, 2005).

In lieu of these trends which lead away from counseling, we have previously discussed in the fourth chapter that coping mechanisms against acculturative stress among Asian Americans have largely been found to be developed through peer networks such as racial/ethnic student organizations (Inkelas, 2004; Museus, 2008). Similar patterns also have been found to be true for Asian international students, and especially if such peer networks contain American students. Interacting with American students in informal settings has been shown to aid the acculturation process for international students more so than simply establishing social networks with co-national students (Heggins & Jackson, 2003; Lee, Park, & Kim, 2009). While obviously there are some issues of mental health which only professional counseling will be able to address effectively, providing safe spaces for international students to acculturate to a holistic campus climate may ease many of the perceived stigmas they hold regarding belonging to the university or its student body, particularly in predominantly White, American institutions.

Beyond contextualizing the past and present geographic location of Asian international students, the literature on Asian American educational experiences also helps us understand that classification and analysis of Asian international students based on their academic demographics are also vital in guiding professional practice in postsecondary institutions. Forty-one percent of international students are currently pursuing degrees in STEM fields, an average which takes into consideration that 42.2% of Chinese students and 74.6% of Indian students are enrolled within STEM. Furthermore, international students are fairly evenly distributed between undergraduates and graduates, with approximately 300,000 students at each academic level. Asian international students reflect a similar distribution with 311,204 graduate students and 271,943 undergraduates (Institute of International Education, 2013). These ratios are in stark contrast to the overall American student population, which contains more than six times as many undergraduates as graduate students (National Center for Education Statistics, 2012). Understanding the academic placement of Asian international students should directly influence the theoretical approaches that educational professionals apply in settings that are both exclusive to international students and integrated within the university at large.

Thus, framing one's approaches to working with Asian international students within the context of the student's cognitive potential, academic/professional aspirations, and social obligations provides a more holistic foundation than the binary frameworks of foreign versus domestic or East versus West that homogenize Asian and Asian American student experiences. These approaches to research, theory, and pedagogical practice within the university environment are not just exclusive to this particular racial/ethnic population, but rather reflect a direct application of the long-term ideals of higher education to a student body that is increasingly reflecting the demographics of our global society.

Concluding Thoughts

As this monograph has revealed, whether AAPIs have lived in the United States for multiple generations or have recently arrived as immigrants, similarities in experiences indicate that there are degrees of racialization that come with looking "Asian," and that resultant campus practices and policies sometimes reflect the inaccuracies embedded in stereotypes. Most notably, the recent admissions debates on the flagship campuses of our public universities have polarized debates about AAPI overrepresentation. The current diversity moment requires a deepened understanding of why and how race (still) matters and that the reinforcement of diversity as a compelling interest serves to advance all students.

References

Abelmann, N. (2009). *The intimate university: Korean American students and the problems of segregation*. Durham, NC: Duke University Press.

Ahn, A. J., Kim, B. S., & Park, Y. S. (2008). Asian cultural values gap, cognitive flexibility, coping strategies, and parent-child conflicts among Korean Americans. *Cultural Diversity and Ethnic Minority Psychology, 14*(4), 353–363.

Alexander v. Holmes County Board of Education, 396 U.S. 19 (1969).

Alvarez, A. N. (2002). Racial identity and Asian Americans: Supports and challenges. In M. K. McEwen, C. M. Kodama, A. N. Lee, S. Lee, & C. T. H. Liang (Eds.), *New Directions for Student Services: No. 97. Working with Asian American college students* (pp. 33–44). San Francisco, CA: Jossey-Bass.

Alvarez, A. N., & Helms, J. E. (2001). Racial identity and reflected appraisals as influences on Asian Americans' racial adjustment. *Cultural Diversity and Ethnic Minority Psychology, 7*, 217–231.

Ancheta, A. N. (1997). *Race, rights, and the Asian American experience*. New Brunswick, NJ: Rutgers University Press.

Ancis, J. R., Sedlacek, W. E., & Mohr, J. J. (2000). Student perceptions of campus cultural climate by race. *Journal of Counseling & Development, 78*(2), 180–185.

Andal, K. C. S. (2002). *The Filipino pensionado experience: Educational opportunity at the university of Illinois at Urbana-Champaign, 1904–1925* (Master's thesis). University of Illinois at Urbana-Champaign, Urbana, IL.

Anderson, J. D. (2007). Race-conscious educational policies versus a "color-blind Constitution": A historical perspective. *Educational Researcher, 36*(5), 249–257.

Anderson, T. H. (2005). The strange career of affirmative action. *South Central Review, 22*(2), 110–129.

Andrews, M. M., & Chun, J. (2007). (Mis)educating about "mixed race": Discourse on multiraciality and the prospects of higher education policy. *Asian American Policy Review, 16*, 87–94.

Aoki, A., & Takeda, O. (2008). *Asian American politics*. Boston, MA: Polity.

Aoki v. Deane. *Petition for Writ of Mandate* (Supreme Court of the State of California, San Francisco, 1907).

Asher, N. (2008). Listening to hyphenated Americans: Hybrid identities of youth from immigrant families. *Theory Into Practice, 47*(1), 12–19.

Asian & Pacific Islander Institute on Domestic Violence (APIIDV). (2010). *Census data & API identities.* Retrieved from http://www.apiidv.org/resources/census-data-api-identities.php#apiEthnicities

Austin, A.W. (2007). *From concentration camp to campus: Japanese American students and World War II.* Urbana: University of Illinois Press.

Balón, D. G. (2003). *Asian Pacific American leadership development.* Leadership Insights and Applications Series No. 14. College Park, MD: National Clearinghouse for Leadership Programs.

Balón, D. G. (2005, April 26). Asian Pacific American college students on leadership: Culturally marginalized from the leader role? *National Association of Student Personnel Administrators (NASPA) NetResults.* Retrieved from http://daniello.balon-home.net/Balon_APAs_Leadership.pdf

Balón, D. G., & Shek, Y. L. (2013). Beyond representation: Confronting the new frontier for Asian American leadership. In S. D. Museus, D. C. Maramba, & R. T. Teranishi (Eds.), *The misrepresented minority: New insights on Asian Americans and Pacific Islanders, and the implications for higher education* (pp. 322–326). Sterling, VA: Stylus.

Bell, D. A. (1993). *Faces at the bottom of the well: The permanence of racism.* New York, NY: Basic Books.

Bonilla-Silva, E. (2009). *Racism without racists: Color-blind racism and the persistence of racial inequality in America* (3rd ed.). Lanham, MD: Rowman & Littlefield.

Bow, L. (2010). *Partly colored: Asian Americans and racial anomaly in the segregated South.* New York: New York University Press.

Bowen, W. G., & Bok, D. (1998). *The shape of the river: Long-term consequences of considering race in college and university admissions.* Princeton, NJ: Princeton University Press.

Brand, D. (1987, August 31). The new whiz kids: Why Asian-Americans are doing so well, and what it costs them. *Time,* 42–47.

Brown v. Board of Education of Topeka, KS, et. al., 347 U.S. 483 (1954).

Buenavista, T. L. (2010). Issues affecting U.S. Filipino student access to postsecondary education: A critical race theory perspective. *Journal of Education for Students Placed at Risk, 15*(1), 114–126. doi:10.1080/10824661003635093

Buenavista, T. L., Jayakumar, U. M., & Misa-Escalante, K. (2009). Contextualizing Asian American education through critical race theory: An example of U.S. Pilipino college student experiences. In S. D. Museus (Ed.), *New Directions for Institutional Research: No. 142. Conducting research on Asian Americans in higher education* (pp. 69–81). San Francisco, CA: Jossey-Bass.

Chan, S. (1991). *Asian Americans: An interpretive history.* Boston, MA: Twayne.

Chan, S., & Wang, L. L. (1991). Racism and the model minority: Asian Americans in higher education. In P. G. Altbach & K. Lomotey (Eds.), *The racial crisis in American higher education* (pp. 43–68). Albany: State University of New York Press.

Chang, E. S., Heckhausen, J., Greenberger, E., & Chen, C. (2009). Shared agency with parents for educational goals: Ethnic differences and implications for college adjustment. *Journal of Youth Adolescence, 39,* 1293–1304.

Chang, J. C. (2005). Faculty student interaction at the community college: A focus on students of color. *Research in Higher Education, 46*(7), 769–802.

Chang, M. J. (2002). Preservation or transformation: Where's the real educational discourse on diversity? *The Review of Higher Education, 25*(2), 125–140.

Chang, M. J., & Kiang, P. N. (2002). New challenges of representing Asian American students in US higher education. In W. A. Smith, P. G. Altbach, & K. Lomotey (Eds.), *The racial crisis in American higher education: Continuing challenges for the twenty-first century* (pp. 137–158). Albany: State University of New York Press.

Chang, M. J., & Kiang, P. N. (2009). AAPI Nexus special issue on higher education. *AAPI Nexus, 7*(2), v–xi.

Chang, M. J., Park, J. J., Lin, M. H., Poon, O. A., & Nakanishi, D. T. (2007). *Beyond myths: The growth and diversity of Asian American college freshmen: 1971–2005.* Los Angeles: Higher Education Research Institute, UCLA.

Chang, R. S. (1993). Toward an Asian American legal scholarship: Critical race theory, post-structuralism, and narrative space. *California Law Review, 81*, 1243–1323.

Chang, R. S. (1999). *Disoriented: Asian Americans, law, and the nation-state.* New York: New York University Press.

Chang, T., & Chang, R. (2004). Counseling and the internet: Asian American and Asian international college students' attitudes toward seeking online professional psychological help. *Journal of College Counseling, 7*, 140–149.

Chen, B., Johnson, A. B., & Takesue, K. (2007). Identity-based discussion groups: A means of providing outreach and support for Asian Pacific American students. *Journal of College Counseling, 10*, 184–192.

Chen, S., Sullivan, N. Y., Lu, Y. E., & Shibusawa, T. (2003). Asian Americans and mental health services: A study of utilization patterns in the 1990's. *Journal of Ethnic and Cultural Diversity in Social Work, 12*(2), 19–42.

Cheng, J. K. Y., Fancher, T. L., Ratanasen, M., Conner, K. R., Duberstein, P. R., Sue, S., & Takeuchi, D. (2010). Lifetime suicidal ideation and suicide attempts in Asian Americans. *Asian American Journal of Psychology, 1*(1), 18–30.

Chew-Ogi, C., & Ogi, A. Y. (2002). Epilogue. In M. K. McEwen, C. M. Kodama, A. N. Lee, S. Lee, & C. T. H. Liang (Eds.), *New Directions for Student Services: No. 97. Working with Asian American college students* (pp. 91–96). San Francisco, CA: Jossey-Bass.

Chhuon, V., & Hudley, C. (2008). Factors supporting Cambodian American students' successful adjustment into the university. *Journal of College Student Development, 49*(1), 15–30.

Chinese Educational Mission. (n.d.). *Origins of the Chinese Educational Mission.* Retrieved from http://www.cemconnections.org/index.php?option=com_content&task=view&id=29&Itemid=34

Choi, Y. (2008). Diversity within: Subgroup differences of youth problem behaviors among Asian Pacific Islander American adolescents. *Journal of Community Psychology, 36*(3), 352–370.

Coloma, R. S. (2006). Disorienting race and education: Changing paradigms on the schooling of Asian Americans and Pacific Islanders. *Race Ethnicity and Education, 9*(1), 1–15.

Crenshaw, K., Gotanda, N., & Peller, G. (1996). *Critical race theory: The key writings that formed the movement.* New York, NY: New Press.

Cress, C. M., & Ikeda, E. K. (2003). Distress under duress: The relationship between campus climate and depression in Asian American college students. *Journal of Student Affairs Research and Practice, 40*(2), 260–283.

Daniels, R. (2003). Educating youth in America's wartime detention camps. *History of Education Quarterly, 43*(1), 91–102.

Delgado, R., & Stefancic, J. (1999). *Critical race theory* (2nd ed.). Philadephia, PA: Temple University Press.

Delgado, R., & Stefancic, J. (2011). *Critical race theory: An introduction.* New York: New York University Press.

Diaz, V. M. (2010). *Repositioning the missionary: Rewriting the histories of colonialism, native Catholicism, and indigeneity in Guam.* Honolulu: University of Hawaii Press.

Douglass, J. (2007). *The conditions for admission: Access, equity, and the social contract of public universities.* Stanford, CA: Stanford University Press.

Dundes, L., Cho, E., & Kwak, S. (2009). The duty to succeed: Honor versus happiness in college and career choices of East Asian students in the United States. *Pastoral Care in Education, 27*(2), 135–156.

Einarson, M. K., & Clarkberg, M. E. (2010). Race differences in the impact of students' out-of-class interactions with faculty. *Journal of the Professoriate, 3*(2), 101–136.

Einarson, M. K., & Matier, M. W. (2005). Exploring race differences in correlates of seniors' satisfaction with undergraduate education. *Research in Higher Education, 46*(6), 641–676.

Espenshade, T. J., & Chung, C. Y. (2005). The opportunity cost of admission preferences at elite universities. *Social Science Quarterly, 86*(2), 293–305.

Espenshade, T. J., & Radford, A. W. (2009). *No longer separate, not yet equal: Race and class in elite college admissions and campus life.* Princeton, NJ: Princeton University Press.

Espiritu, A. F. (2005). *Five faces of exile: The nation and Filipino American intellectuals.* Stanford, CA: Stanford University Press.

Espiritu, Y. L. (1993). *Asian American panethnicity: Bridging institutions and identities.* Philadelphia, PA: Temple University Press.

Espiritu, Y. L. (2001). Possibilities of a multiracial America. In T. Williams-Leon & C. Nakashima (Eds.), *The sum of our parts: Mixed heritage Asian Americans* (pp. 25–34). Philadelphia, PA: Temple University Press.

Fisher v. University of Texas at Austin, 133 S.Ct. 2411 (2013).

Garrod, A., & Kilkenny, R. (2007). *Balancing two worlds: Asian American college students tell their life stories.* Ithaca, NY: Cornell University Press.

George-Jackson, C. E. (2011). STEM switching: Examining departures of undergraduate women in STEM fields. *Journal of Women and Minorities in Science and Engineering, 17*(2), 149–171.

Gim Chung, R. H. (2001). Gender, ethnicity, and acculturation in intergenerational conflict of Asian American college students. *Cultural Diversity and Ethnic Minority Psychology, 7*, 376–386.

Gloria, A. M., & Ho, T. A. (2003). Environmental, social, and psychological experiences of Asian American undergraduates: Examining issues of academic persistence. *Journal of Counseling & Development, 81*, 93–105.

Gonzalez, A. (2012). Redefining racial paradigms: Asian American Greek letter organizations in American higher education. In A. Agbayani & D. Ching (Eds.), *Asian Americans and Pacific Islanders in higher education* (pp. 213–229). Washington, DC: NASPA.

Gorelick, S. (1981). *City college and the Jewish poor: Education in New York, 1880–1924.* New Brunswick, NJ: Rutgers University Press.

Goza, F., & Ryabov, I. (2009). Adolescents' educational outcomes: Racial and ethnic variations in peer network importance. *Journal of Youth & Adolescence, 38*(9), 1264–1279.

Gratz v. Bollinger, 539 U.S. 244 (2003).

Grutter v. Bollinger, 539 U.S. 306 (2003).

Gurin, P., Dey, E. L., Hurtado, S., & Gurin, G. (2002). Diversity and higher education: Theory and impact on educational outcomes. *Harvard Educational Review, 72*(3), 330–367.

Gurin, P., Nagda, B. R. A., & Lopez, G. E. (2004). The benefits of diversity in education for democratic citizenship. *Journal of Social Issues, 60*(1), 17–34.

Han, M., & Lee, M. (2011). Risk and protective factors contributing to depressive symptoms in Vietnamese American college students. *Journal of College Student Development, 52*(2), 154–166.

Harper, S. R., & Hurtado, S. (2007). Nine themes in campus racial climates and implications for institutional transformation. In S. R. Harper & L. D. Patton (Eds.), *New Directions for Institutional Research: No. 120. Responding to the realities of race on campus* (pp. 7–24). San Francisco, CA: Jossey-Bass.

Hartlep, N. D. (2013). *The model minority stereotype: Demystifying Asian American success*. Charlotte, NC: Information Age Press.

Heggins, W. J., & Jackson, J. F. (2003). Understanding the collegiate experience for Asian international students at a Midwestern research university. *College Student Journal, 37*(3), 379–391.

Hing, B. O. (1993). *Making and remaking Asian America through immigration policy, 1850–1990*. Stanford, CA: Stanford University Press.

Ho v. San Francisco Unified School District, Nos. 97–15926, 97–70378 (1998).

Hong, G. K. (2011). *Strange affinities: The gender and sexual politics of comparative racialization*. Durham, NC: Duke University Press.

Horn, R. A., & Ethington, C. A. (2002). Self-reported beliefs of community college students regarding their growth and development: Ethnic and enrollment status differences. *Community College Journal of Research and Practice, 26*(5), 401–413.

Hsia, J., & Hirano-Nakanishi, M. (1989). The demographics of diversity: Asian Americans and higher education. *Change: The Magazine of Higher Learning, 21*(6), 20–27.

Huang, C. (2001). *The soft power of U.S. education and the formation of a Chinese American intellectual community in Urbana-Champaign, 1905–1954* (Doctoral dissertation). University of Illinois at Urbana-Champaign, Urbana, IL.

Huang, K. (2012). Asian American mental health on campus. In A. Agbayani & D. Ching (Eds.), *Asian Americans and Pacific Islanders in higher education* (pp. 231–250). Washington, DC: NASPA.

Hune, S. (2002). Demographics and diversity of Asian American college students. In M. K. McEwen, C. M. Kodama, A. N. Alvarez, S. Lee, & C. T. H. Liang (Eds.), *New Directions for Student Services: No. 97. Working with Asian American college students* (pp. 11–20). San Francisco, CA: Jossey-Bass.

Hune, S. (2006). Asian Pacific American women and men in higher education: Contested spaces of their participation, persistence, and challenges as students, faculty, and administrators. In G. Li & G. H. Beckett (Eds.), *Strangers of the academy: Asian women scholars in higher education* (pp. 15–36). Sterling, VA: Stylus.

Hune, S. (2011). Educational data, research methods, policies, and practices that matter for AAPIs. *AAPI Nexus: Asian Americans & Pacific Islanders Policy, Practice and Community*, 9(1), 115–118.

Hurtado, S. (2007). Linking diversity with the educational and civic missions of higher education. *The Review of Higher Education, 30*(2), 185–196.

Hurtado, S., Milem, J., Clayton-Pedersen, A., & Allen, W. (1999). *Enacting diverse learning environments: Improving the climate for racial/ethnic diversity in higher education* [ASHE-Eric Higher Education Report, 26(8)]. Washington, DC: Graduate School of Education and Human Development, The George Washington University.

Hwang, W., & Goto, S. (2009). The impact of perceived racial discrimination on the mental health of Asian American and Latino college students. *Asian American Journal of Psychology, S*(1), 15–28.

Hyun, J. K., Quinn, B. C., Madon, T., & Lustig, S. (2006). Graduate student mental health: Needs assessment and utilization of counseling services. *Journal of College Student Development, 47*(3), 247–266.

Ibrahim, F., Ohnishi, H., & Sandhu, D. S. (1997). Asian American identity development: A culture specific model for South Asian Americans. *Journal of Multicultural Counseling and Development, 25*, 34–50.

Ignatiev, N. (2008). *How the Irish became White*. New York, NY: Routledge.

Inkelas, K. K. (2004). Does participation in ethnic cocurricular activities facilitate a sense of ethnic awareness and understanding? A study of Asian Pacific American undergraduates. *Journal of College Student Development, 45*, 285–302.

Institute of International Education. (2013). *Open Doors data*. Retrieved from http://www.iie.org/en/Research-and-Publications/Open-Doors/Data

Ito, L. A. (2000). Japanese American women and the student relocation movement, 1942–1945. *Frontiers: A Journal of Women Studies, 21*(3), 1–24.

Iwamoto, D. K., Corbin, W., & Fromme, K. (2010). Trajectory classes of heavy episodic drinking among Asian American college students. *Addiction, 105*, 1912–1920.

James, T. (1987). *Exile within: The schooling of Japanese Americans*. Cambridge, MA: Harvard University Press.

Joseph, P. E. (2006). *Waiting'til the midnight hour: A narrative history of Black power in America*. New York, NY: Henry Holt and Company.

Joshi, K. Y. (2006). *New roots in America's sacred ground: Religion, race, and ethnicity in Indian America*. New Brunswick, NJ: Rutgers University Press.

Kang, J. (1996). Negative action against Asian Americans: The internal instability of Dworkin's defense of affirmative action. *Harvard Civil Rights-Civil Liberties Law Review, 31*, 1–47.

Kao, G. (1995). Asian Americans as model minorities? A look at their academic performance. *American Journal of Education, 103*(2), 121–159.

Kao, G., & Thompson, J. (2003). Racial and ethnic stratification in educational achievement and attainment. *Annual Review of Sociology, 29*, 417–442.

Karabel, J. (2005). *The chosen: The hidden history of admission and exclusion at Harvard, Yale, and Princeton*. Boston, MA: Houghton Mifflin Company.

Kawaguchi, S. (2003). Ethnic identity development and collegiate experience of Asian Pacific American students: Implications for practice. *NASPA Journal, 40*(3), 13–29.

Kearney, L., Draper, M., & Baron, A. (2005). Counseling utilization by ethnic minority college students. *Cultural Diversity and Ethnic Minority Psychology, 11*(3), 272–285.

Khanna, N. (2004). The role of reflected appraisals in racial identity: The case of multiracial Asians. *Social Psychology Quarterly, 67*(2), 115–131.

Kibria, N. (1999). College and notions of "Asian American": Second-generation Chinese and Korean Americans negotiate race and identity. *Amerasia Journal, 25*, 29–51.

Kidder, W. C. (2005). Negative action versus affirmative action: Asian Pacific Americans are still caught in the crossfire. *Michigan Journal of Race & Law, 11*, 606–624.

Kim, C. J. (1999). The racial triangulation of Asian Americans. *Politics & Society, 27*(1), 105–138.

Kim, C. J. (2003). *Bitter fruit: The politics of Black-Korean conflict in New York City.* New Haven, CT: Yale University Press.

Kim, D. (2004). The effect of financial aid on students' college choice: Differences by racial groups. *Research in Higher Education, 45*(1), 43–70.

Kim, E., & Lee, D. (2011). Collective self-esteem: Role of social context among Asian-American college students. *Psychological Reports, 109*(3), 1017–1037.

Kim, J. (2001). Asian American identity development theory. In C. L. Wijeyesinghe & B. W. Jackson, III (Eds.), *New perspectives on racial identity development: A theoretical and practical anthology* (pp. 67–90). New York: New York University Press.

Kim, J. K., & Gasman, M. (2011). In search of a "good college": Decisions and determinations behind Asian American students' college choice. *Journal of College Student Development, 52*(6), 706–728.

Kisch, J., Leino, E. V., & Silverman, M. M. (2005). Aspects of suicidal behavior, depression and treatment in college students: Results from the spring 2000 National College Health Assessment Survey. *Suicide and Life-Threatening Behavior, 35*, 3–13.

Kitano, H. H. L. (1993). *Generations and identity: Japanese Americans.* Needham, MA: Ginn Press.

Kodama, C. M., & Abreo, A. (2009). Do labels matter? Attitudinal and behavioral correlates of ethnic and racial identity choices among Asian American undergraduates. *The College Student Affairs Journal, 27*(2), 155–175.

Kodama, C. M., McEwen, M. K., Liang, C. T. H., & Lee, S. (2002). An Asian American perspective on psychosocial student development theory. In M. K. McEwen, C. M. Kodama, A. N. Alvarez, S. Lee, & C. T. H. Liang (Eds.), *New Directions for Student Services: No. 97. Working with Asian American college students* (pp. 45–59). San Francisco, CA: Jossey-Bass.

Kurashige, S. (2007). *The shifting grounds of race: Black and Japanese Americans in the making of multiethnic Los Angeles.* Princeton, NJ: Princeton University Press.

Kwon, Y. (2009). Factors affecting international students' transition to higher education institutions in the United States—From the perspective of office of international students. *College Student Journal, 43*(4), 1020–1036.

Laanan, F. S., & Starobin, S. S. (2004). Defining Asian and Pacific Islander serving institutions. In B. V. Laden (Ed.), *New Directions for Community Colleges: No. 127. Serving minority populations* (pp. 49–59). San Francisco, CA: Jossey-Bass.

Ladson-Billings, G., & Tate, W. F. (1995). Toward a critical race theory of education. *Teachers College Record, 97*(1), 47–68.

Lee, E. (2007). The "yellow peril" and Asian exclusion in the Americas. *Pacific Historical Review, 76*(4), 537–562.

Lee, R. M., & Liu, H. T. (2001). Coping with intergenerational family conflict: Comparison of Asian American, Hispanic, and European American college students. *Journal of Counseling Psychology, 48*(4), 410–419.

Lee, R. M., Su, J., & Yoshida, E. (2005). Coping with intergenerational family conflict among Asian American college students. *Journal of Counseling Psychology, 52*(3), 389–399.

Lee, S. A., Park, H. S., & Kim, W. (2009). Gender differences in international students' adjustment. *College Student Journal, 43*(4), 1217–1227.

Lee, S. C. (2007). The self-rated social well-being of Hmong college students in Northern California. *Hmong Studies Journal, 8*, 1–19.

Lee, S. J. (1996). *Unraveling the "model minority" stereotype: Listening to Asian American youth.* New York, NY: Teachers College Press, Columbia University.

Lee, S. J. (2005). *Up against whiteness: Race, school, and immigrant youth.* New York, NY: Teachers College Press, Columbia University.

Lee, S. S. (2006). Over-represented and de-minoritized: The racialization of Asian Americans in higher education. *InterActions: UCLA Journal of Education and Information Studies, 2*(2), 1–15.

Lee, S. S. (2008). De-minoritization of Asian Americans: A historical examination of the representations of Asian Americans in affirmative action admissions policies at the university of California. *Asian American Law Journal, 15*, 129–152.

Lee, S. S. (2010). *(Un)seen and (un)heard: The struggle for Asian American "minority" recognition at the University of Illinois at Urbana-Champaign, 1968–1997* (Doctoral dissertation). University of Illinois at Urbana-Champaign, Urbana, IL.

Lei, J. L. (2003). (Un)necessary toughness?: Those "loud Black girls" and those "quiet Asian boys." *Anthropology & Education Quarterly, 34*(2), 158–181.

Levine, D. O. (1986). *The American college and the culture of aspiration, 1915–1940.* Ithaca, NY: Cornell University Press.

Lew, J. (2006a). *Asian Americans in class: Charting the achievement gap among Korean American youth.* New York, NY: Teachers College Press.

Lew, J. (2006b). Burden of acting neither White nor Black: Asian American identities and achievement in urban schools. *Urban Review, 38*(5), 335–352.

Lew, J. W., Chang, J. C., & Wang, W. W. (2005). UCLA community college review: The overlooked minority: Asian Pacific American students at community colleges. *Community College Review, 33*(2), 64–84.

Liang, C. T. H., Lee, S., Ting, M. P. (2002). Developing Asian American leaders. In M. K. McEwen, C. M. Kodama, A. N. Alvarez, S. Lee, & C. T. H. Liang (Eds.), *New Directions for Student Services: No. 97. Working with Asian American college students* (pp. 81–89). San Francisco, CA: Jossey-Bass.

Liang, C. T. H., & Sedlacek, W. (2003). Attitudes of White student services practitioners toward Asian Americans. *NASPA Journal, 40*(3), 30–42.

Literte, P. E. (2010). Revising race: How biracial students are changing and challenging student services. *Journal of College Student Development, 51*(2), 115–134.

Loewen, J. W. (1971). *The Mississippi Chinese: Between Black and White.* Cambridge, MA: Harvard University Press.

Louie, V. (2001). Parents' aspirations and investment: The role of social class in the educational experiences of 1.5- and second-generation Chinese Americans. *Harvard Educational Review, 71*(3), 438–474.

Low, V. (1982). *The unimpressible race. A century of educational struggle by the Chinese in San Francisco.* San Francisco, CA: East/West Publishing Company.

Lowe, S. M. (2005). Integrating collectivist values into career counseling with Asian Americans: A test of cultural responsiveness. *Journal of Multicultural Counseling and Development, 33,* 134–145.

Lum v. Rice, 275 U.S. 78 (1927).

Ly, P. (2008). Caught between two cultures. *Diverse: Issues in Higher Education, 25*(14), 24–25.

Major, E. M. (2005). Co-national support, cultural therapy, and the adjustment of Asian students to an English-speaking university culture. *International Education Journal, 6*(1), 84–95.

Mallinckrodt, B., Shigeoka, S., & Suzuki, L. A. (2005). Asian and Pacific Island American students' acculturation and etiology beliefs about typical counseling presenting problems. *Cultural Diversity and Ethnic Minority Psychology, 11*(3), 227–238.

Maramba, D. C. (2008a). Immigrant families and the college experience: Perspectives of Filipina Americans. *Journal of College Student Development, 49*(4), 336–350.

Maramba, D. C. (2008b). Understanding campus climate through the voices of Filipina/o American college students. *College Student Journal, 42*(4), 1045–1060.

Maramba, D. C. (2011a). Few and far between: Exploring the experiences of Asian American and Pacific Islander women in student affairs administration. In G. Jean-Marie, B. Lloyd-Jones, & L. Bass (Eds.), *Women of color in higher education: Turbulent past, promising future* (pp. 337–359). Bingley, UK: Emerald Group Publishing.

Maramba, D. C. (2011b). The importance of critically disaggregating data: The case of Southeast Asian American college students. *AAPI Nexus, 9*(1/2), 127–133.

Maramba, D. C. (2013a). Family and education environments: Contexts and counterstories of Filipino Americans. In R. Endo & X. L. Rong (Eds.), *Educating Asian Americans: Achievement, schooling, and identities* (pp. 205–231). Charlotte, NC: Information Age Publishing.

Maramba, D. C. (2013b). Creating successful pathways for Asian Americans and Pacific Islander (AAPI) community college students in STEM. In R. Palmer & L. Wood (Eds.), *Community college and STEM: Examining underrepresented racial and ethnic minorities* (pp. 156–171). New York, NY: Routledge.

Maramba, D. C., & Bonus, R. (Eds.). (2013). *The other students: Filipino Americans, education and power.* Charlotte, NC: Information Age Publishing.

Maramba, D. C., & Museus, S. D. (2011). The utility of using mixed methods and intersectionality approaches in conducting research on Filipino American students' experiences with campus climates and sense of belonging. In K. A. Griffin & S. D. Museus (Eds.), *New Directions for Institutional Research: No. 151. Using mixed methods to study intersectionality in higher education* (pp. 93–101). San Francisco, CA: Jossey-Bass.

Maramba, D. C., & Museus, S. D. (2012). Examining the effects of campus climate, ethnic group cohesion and cross cultural interaction on Filipino American students' sense of belonging in college. *Journal of College Student Retention, 15*(1), 495–522.

Maramba, D. C., & Nadal, K. L. Y. (2013). The state of Filipino/a American faculty: Implications for higher education. In D. C. Maramba & R. Bonus (Eds.), *The other students: Filipino Americans, education and power* (pp. 297–307). Charlotte, NC: Information Age Publishing, Inc.

Maramba, D. C., & Palmer, R. T. (in press). The role of cultural validation in the college experience of Southeast Asian American college students. *Journal of College Student Development.*

Matsuda, M. J., Lawrence, C., Delgado, R., & Crenshaw, K. (1993). *Words that wound: Critical race theory, assaultive speech, and the first amendment.* Boulder, CO: Westview Press.

Matsumoto, V. (1984). Japanese American women during World War II. *Frontiers: A Journal of Women Studies, 8*(1), 6–14.

McEwen, M. K., Kodama, C. M., Alvarez, A. N., Lee, S., & Liang, C. T. H. (Eds.). (2002). *New Directions for Student Services: No. 97. Working with Asian American college students.* San Francisco, CA: Jossey-Bass.

Meekyung, H. (2005). Relationship among perceived parental trauma, parental attachment, and sense of coherence in Southeast Asian American college students. *Journal of Family Social Work, 9*(2), 25–45.

Métraux, D. A. (2010). *Jack London, Asian wars and the "Yellow Peril."* Retrieved from http://hnn.us/article/123122

Milem, J. F., Clayton-Pedersen, A. R., Hurtado, S., & Allen, W. R. (1998). Enhancing campus climates for racial/ethnic diversity: Educational policy and practice. *The Review of Higher Education, 21*(3), 279–302.

Miville, M. L., & Constantine, M. G. (2007). Cultural values, counseling stigma, and intentions to seek counseling among Asian American college women. *Counseling and Values, 52,* 2–11.

Moynihan, D. P. (1965). *The Negro family: The case for national action.* Washington, DC: Department of Labor, Office of Policy Planning, & Research.

Museus, S. D. (2008). The role of ethnic student organizations in fostering African American and Asian American students' cultural adjustment and membership at predominantly White institutions. *Journal of College Student Development, 59*(6), 568–586.

Museus, S. D. (Ed.). (2009). *New Directions for Institutional Research: No. 142. Conducting research on Asian Americans in higher education.* San Francisco, CA: Jossey-Bass.

Museus, S. D., & Chang, M. J. (2009). Rising to the challenge of conducting research on Asian Americans in higher education. In S. D. Museus (Ed.), *New Directions for Institutional Research: No. 142. Conducting research on Asian Americans in higher education* (pp. 95–105). San Francisco, CA: Jossey-Bass.

Museus, S. D., & Maramba, D. C. (2011). The impact of culture on Filipino American students' sense of belonging. *Review of Higher Education, 34*(2), 231–258.

Museus, S. D., Maramba, D. C., Palmer, R. T., Reyes, A., & Bresonis, K. (2013). An explanatory model of Southeast Asian American college student success: A grounded theory analysis. Asian Americans. In R. Endo & X. L. Rong (Eds.), *Educating Asian Americans: Achievement, schooling, and identities* (pp. 1–28). Charlotte, NC: Information Age Publishing.

Museus, S. D., Maramba, D. C., & Teranishi, R. T. (Eds.). (2013). *The misrepresented minority: New insights on Asian Americans and Pacific Islanders and their implications for higher education.* Sterling, VA: Stylus.

Museus, S. D., Palmer, R. T., Davis, R. J., & Maramba, D. C. (2011). *Racial and ethnic minority students' success in STEM education* [ASHE-Higher Education Report Series, 36(6)]. San Francisco, CA: Jossey-Bass.

Nadal, K. L. (2004). Pilipino American identity model. *Journal of Multicultural Counseling and Development, 32*(1), 44–61.

Nadal, K. L., Pituc, S. T., Johnston, M. P., & Esparrago, T. (2010). Overcoming the model minority myth: Experiences of Filipino American graduate students. *Journal of College Student Development, 51*(6), 1–13.

Nakanishi, D. T. (1989). A quota on excellence? The Asian American admissions debate. *Change: The Magazine of Higher Learning, 21*(6), 39–47.

Nakanishi, D. T. (1993). Asian Pacific Americans in higher education: Faculty and administrative representation and tenure. In J. Gainen and R. Boice (Eds.), *New Directions for Teaching and Learning: No. 53. Building a diverse faculty* (pp. 51–59). San Francisco, CA: Jossey-Bass.

Nakanishi, D. T., & Nishida, T. Y. (1995). *The Asian American educational experience: A source book for teachers and students.* New York, NY: Routledge.

Narui, M. (2011). Understanding Asian/American gay, lesbian, and bisexual experiences from a poststructural perspective. *Journal of Homosexuality, 58,* 1211–1234.

National Center for Education Statistics. (2012). *Integrated Postsecondary Education Data Sets* [Data file]. Retrieved from http://nces.eg.gov/ipeds

National Commission on Asian American and Pacific Islander Research in Education (CARE). (2008). *Asian Americans and Pacific Islanders facts, not fiction: Setting the record straight.* New York, NY: Author.

National Commission on Asian American and Pacific Islander Research in Education (CARE). (2010). *Federal higher education policy priorities and the Asian American and Pacific Islander community.* New York, NY: Author.

National Commission on Asian American and Pacific Islander Research in Education (CARE). (2011). *The relevance of Asian Americans & Pacific Islanders in the college completion agenda.* New York, NY: Author.

National Education Association (NEA). (2008). *Focus on Asian Americans and Pacific Islanders.* Washington, DC: Author.

Ng, J. C., Lee, S. S., & Pak, Y. K. (2007). Contesting the model minority and perpetual foreigner stereotypes: A critical review of literature on Asian Americans in education. *Review of Research in Education, 31*(1), 95–130.

Ngai, M. M. (2004). *Impossible subjects: Illegal aliens and the making of modern America.* Princeton, NJ: Princeton University Press.

Ngo, B. (2006). Learning from the margins: The education of Southeast and South Asian Americans in context. *Race, Ethnicity, & Education, 9*(1), 51–65.

Ngo, B., & Lee, S. J. (2007). Complicating the image of model minority success: A review of Southeast Asian American education. *Review of Educational Research, 77*(4), 415–453.

O'Brien, R. W. (1949). *The college Nisei.* New York, NY: Arno Press.

Okazaki, S. (2002). Influences of culture on Asian Americans' sexuality. *Journal of Sex Research, 39*(1), 34–41.

Okihiro, G. Y. (1999). *Storied lives: Japanese American students and World War II.* Seattle: University of Washington Press.

Omatsu, G. (2003). The "four prisons" and the movements of liberation: Asian American activism from the 1960s to the 1990s. In D. T. Nakanishi & J. S. Lai (Eds.), *Asian American politics: Law, participation, and policy* (pp. 135–162). Lanham, MD: Rowman & Littlefield.

Omi, M., & Winant, H. (1994). *Racial formation in the United States: From the 1960s to the 1990s.* New York, NY: Routledge.

Ong, A. (2003). *Buddha is hiding: Refugees, citizenship, the new America*. Berkeley: University of California Press.

Ono, K. A., & Pham, V. (2008). *Asian Americans and the media*. Cambridge, UK: Polity.

Orfield, G., & Lee, C. (2007). *Historic reversals, accelerating resegregation, and the need for new integration strategies*. Civil Rights Project. Los Angeles: UCLA.

Orsuwan, M. (2011). Interaction between community college processes and Asian American and Pacific Islander subgroups. *Community College Journal of Research and Practice, 35*(10), 743–755.

Orsuwan, M., & Cole, D. (2007). The moderating effects of race/ethnicity on the experience of Asian American and Pacific Islander community college students. *Asian American Policy Review, 16*, 61–85.

Osajima, K. (1995). Racial politics and the invisibility of Asian Americans in higher education. *Educational Foundations, 9*(1), 35–53.

Osajima, K. (2007). Replenishing the ranks: Raising critical consciousness among Asian Americans. *Journal of Asian American Studies, 10*(1), 59–83.

Otsuki, M. (2009). Social connectedness and smoking behaviors among Asian American college students: An electronic diary study. *Nicotine & Tobacco Research, 11*(4), 418–426.

Pak, Y. K. (2001). *Wherever I go, I will always be a loyal American: Seattle's Japanese American schoolchildren during World War II*. New York, NY: RoutledgeFalmer.

Palmer, R. T., Maramba, D. C., Gasman, M., & Lloyd, K. D. J. (2013). Charting the course. In R. T. Palmer, D. C. Maramba, & M. Gasman (Eds.), *Fostering success of ethnic and racial minorities in STEM: The role of minority serving institutions* (pp. 1–15). New York, NY: Routledge.

Pang, V. O., & Cheng, L. L. (1998). *Struggling to be heard: The unmet needs of Asian Pacific American children*. Albany, NY: SUNY Press.

Pang, V. O., Han, P. P., & Pang, J. M. (2011). Asian American and Pacific Islander students: Equity and the achievement gap. *Educational Researcher, 40*(8), 378–389.

Parents Involved in Community Schools v. Seattle School District No. 1, 551 U.S. 701 (2007).

Park, J. J. (2008). Race and the Greek system in the 21st century: Centering the voices of Asian American women. *NASPA Journal, 45*(1), 103–132.

Park, J. J. (2009). Are we satisfied? A look at student satisfaction with diversity at traditionally White institutions. *The Review of Higher Education, 32*(3), 291–320.

Park, J. J. (2011). "I needed to get out of my Korean bubble": An ethnographic account of Korean American collegians juggling diversity in a religious context. *Anthropology & Education Quarterly, 42*(3), 193–212.

Park, J. J., & Teranishi, R. T. (2008). Asian American and Pacific Islander Serving Institutions: Historical perspectives and future prospects. In M. Gasman, B. Baez, & C. S. Turner (Eds.), *Interdisciplinary approaches to understanding minority serving institutions* (pp. 111–126). Albany, NY: SUNY Press.

Parrenas-Shimizu, C. (2007). *The hypersexuality of race: Performing Asian/American women on screen and scene*. Durham, NC: Duke University Press.

Parrenas-Shimizu, C. (2012). *Straitjacket sexualities: Unbinding Asian American manhoods in the movies*. Palo Alto, CA: Stanford University Press.

Peng, S. S., & Wright, D. (1994). Explanation of academic achievement of Asian American students. *Journal of Educational Research, 87*(6), 346–352.

Pepin, S. C., & Talbot, D. M. (2013). Negotiating the complexities of being self-identified as both Asian American and lesbian, gay, or bisexual. In S. D. Museus, D. C. Maramba, & R. T. Teranishi (Eds.), *The misrepresented minority: New insights on Asian Americans and Pacific Islanders, and the implications for higher education* (pp. 227–243). Sterling, VA: Stylus.

Petersen, W. (1966, January 9). Success story, Japanese-American style. *New York Times Magazine,* 20–43.

Pew Research Center. (2012). *The rise of Asian Americans.* Washington, DC: Author.

Plessy v. Ferguson, 163 U.S. 537 (1896).

Poon, O. A. (2009a). AAPIs in the college access debate: A case of generational and communication gaps in the AAPI education agenda. *AAPI Nexus, 7*(2), 83–105.

Poon, O. A. (2009b). Haunted by negative action: Asian Americans, admissions, and race in the "color-blind era." *Asian American Policy Review, 18,* 81–90.

Posadas, B. M. (2013). Transnationalism and higher education: Four Filipino Chicago case studies. *Journal of American Ethnic History, 32*(2), 7–37.

Posadas, B. M., & Guyotte, R. L. (1990). Unintentional immigrants: Chicago's Filipino foreign students become settlers, 1900–1941. *Journal of American Ethnic History, 9*(2), 26–48.

Posadas, B. M., & Guyotte, R. L. (1992). Aspiration and reality: Occupational and educational choice among Filipino migrants to Chicago, 1900–1935. *Illinois Historical Journal, 85*(2), 89–104.

Poyrazli, S., Kavanaugh, P. R., Baker, A., & Al-Timmi, N. (2004). Social support and demographic correlates of acculturative stress in international students. *Journal of College Counseling, 7,* 73–82.

Regents of the University of California v. Bakke, 438 U.S. 265 (1978).

Rhoads, R. A., Lee, J. J., & Yamada, M. (2002). Panethnicity and collective action among Asian American students: A qualitative case study. *Journal of College Student Development, 43,* 876–891.

Roediger, D. R. (2005). *Working toward whiteness: How America's immigrants became White.* New York, NY: Basic Books.

Roldan v. Los Angeles County, 129 Cal. App. 267 18 P.2d 706 (1933).

Root, M. P. P. (1992). *Racially mixed people in America.* Newbury Park, CA: Sage Publications.

Root, M. P. P. (1997). Multiracial Asians: Models of ethnic identity. *Amerasia Journal, 23*(1), 29–41.

Rorabaugh, W. J. (1990). *Berkeley at war: The 1960s.* New York, NY: Oxford University Press.

Rosenfeld, S. (2012). *Subversives: The FBI's war on student radicals and Reagan's rise to power.* New York, NY: Farrar, Straus, and Giroux.

Rudolph, F. (1962). *The American college and university: A history.* New York, NY: Vintage Books.

Schuette v. Coalition to Defend Affirmative Action, No. 12–682 (2013).

Shek, Y. L., & McEwen, M. K. (2012). The relationships of racial identity and gender role conflict to self-esteem of Asian American undergraduate men. *Journal of College Student Development, 53*(5), 703–718.

Sikh Coalition, Asian American Legal Defense and Education Fund (AALDEF), and the New York Civil Liberties Union (NYCLU). (2010). *Bullying in New York city schools: Educators speak out, 2009–2010.* New York, NY: Author.

Smith, T. D. (2010). *Asian American/European American and Latino/a/European American multiracial psychology students in higher education: Academic barriers, academic supports, perceptions of cultural diversity, and experiences* (Doctoral dissertation). University of Maryland, Baltimore County, MD.

So, D. W., Wong, F. Y., & DeLeon, J. M. (2005). Sex, HIV risks, and substance use among Asian American college students. *AIDS Education & Prevention, 17*(5), 457–468.

Su, J., Lee, R. M., & Vang, S. (2005). Intergenerational family conflict and coping among Hmong American college students. *Journal of Counseling Psychology, 52*(4), 482–489.

Sue, D. W., Bucceri, J. M., Lin, A. I., Nadal, K. L., & Torino, G. C. (2007). Racial microaggressions and the Asian American experience. *Cultural Diversity and Ethnic Minority Psychology, 13*(1), 72–81.

Sue, S., & McKinney, H. (1975). Asian Americans in the community mental health care system. *American Journal of Orthopsychiatry, 45*(1), 111–118.

Sue, S., Yan Cheng, J. K., Saad, C. S., & Chu, J. P. (2012). Asian American mental health: A call to action. *American Psychologist, 67*(7), 532–544.

Suzuki, B. H. (2002). Revisiting the model minority stereotype: Implications for student affairs practice and higher education. In M. K. McEwen, C. M. Kodama, A. N. Alvarez, S. Lee, & C. T. H. Liang (Eds.), *New Directions for Student Services: No. 97. Working with Asian American college students* (pp. 21–32). San Francisco, CA: Jossey-Bass.

Sweatt v. Painter, 339 U.S. 629 (1950).

Synnott, M. G. (2010). *The half-opened door: Discrimination and admissions at Harvard, Yale, and Princeton, 1900–1970*. Edison, NJ: Transaction.

Takagi, D. Y. (1998). *The retreat from race: Asian-American admissions and racial politics*. New Brunswick, NJ: Rutgers University Press.

Takaki, R. (1989). *Strangers from a different shore: A history of Asian Americans*. Boston, MA: Little Brown.

Takemoto, M. A., & Hayashino, D. (2012). Demystifying mental health for APPI students college campuses. In A. Agbayani & D. Ching (Eds.), *Asian Americans and Pacific Islanders in higher education* (pp. 251–267). Washington, DC: NASPA.

Tamura, E. H. (1993). *Americanization, acculturation, and ethnic identity: The Nisei generation in Hawaii*. Urbana: University of Illinois Press.

Tamura, E. H. (2001). Asian Americans in the history of education: An historiographical essay. *History of Education Quarterly, 41*(1), 58–71.

Tamura, E. H. (2003). Introduction: Asian Americans and educational history. *History of Education Quarterly, 43*(1), 1–9.

Tamura, E. H. (2010). Value messages collide with reality: Joseph Kurihara and the power of informal education. *History of Education Quarterly, 50*(1), 1–33.

Tang, M. (2002). A comparison of Asian American, Caucasian American, and Chinese college students: An initial report. *Multicultural Counseling and Development, 30*, 124–134.

Tape v. Hurley, 66 Cal. 473 (1885).

Teranishi, R. T. (2010). *Asians in the ivory tower: Dilemmas of racial inequality in American higher education*. New York, NY: Teachers College Press.

Teranishi, R. T., Behringer, L. B., Grey, E. A., & Parker, T. L. (2009). Critical race theory and research on Asian Americans and Pacific Islanders in higher education. In S. D. Museus (Ed.), *New Directions for Institutional Research: No. 142. Conducting research on Asian Americans in higher education* (pp. 57–68). San Francisco, CA: Jossey-Bass.

Teranishi, R. T., Maramba, D. C., & Ta, M.-H. (2012). Asian American Native American Pacific Islander Serving Institutions (AANAPISIs): Mutable sites of intervention for STEM opportunities and outcomes. In R. T. Palmer, D. C. Maramba, & M. Gasman (Eds.), *Fostering success of ethnic and racial minorities in STEM: The role of minority serving institutions* (pp. 168–180). New York, NY: Routledge.

Thelin, J. R. (2011). *A history of American higher education.* Baltimore, MD: Johns Hopkins University Press.

Tochkov, K., Levine, L., & Sanaka, A. (2010). Variation in the prediction of cross-cultural adjustment by Asian-Indian students in the United States. *College Student Journal, 44*(3), 677–689.

Tseng, V. (2004). Family interdependence and academic adjustment in college: Youth from immigrant and US-born families. *Child Development, 75*(3), 966–983.

Tuan, M. (1999). *Forever foreigners or honorary Whites? The Asian ethnic experience today.* New Brunswick, NJ: Rutgers University Press.

Uba, L. (2003). *Asian Americans: Personality patterns, identity, and mental health.* Greensboro, NC: Guilford Press.

Umemoto, K. (1989). "On strike!" San Francisco state college strike, 1968–69: The role of Asian American students. *Amerasia Journal, 15*(1), 3–41.

United States v. Bhagat Singh Thind, 261 U.S. 204 (1923).

U.S. Census Bureau. (2010). *2010 Census data results for the Asian population and Native Hawaiian and other Pacific Islander population.* Retrieved from http://www.apiidv.org/files/2010Census-WHIAAPI-2011.pdf

U.S. Census Bureau. (2013). *Asians fastest growing race or ethnic group in 2012, Census Bureau Reports.* Retrieved from http://www.census.gov/newsroom/releases/archives/population/cb13-112.html

U.S. Department of Education. (2010). *Asian American and Native American Pacific Islander Serving Institutions (AANAPISIs) receive $2.6 million in federal grant funding.* Retrieved from http://www.ed.gov/news/press-releases/asian-american-and-native-american-pacific-islander-serving-institutions-aanapis

U.S. Department of Education. (2013). *Asian American and Native American Pacific Islander Serving Institutions program.* Retrieved from http://www2.ed.gov/programs/aanapi/awards.html

U.S. News & World Report. (1966, December 26). Success story of one minority group in U.S., pp. 6–9.

U.S. News & World Report. (2012, December 12). *Most international students.* Retrieved from http://colleges.usnews.rankingsandreviews.com/best-colleges/rankings/national-universities/most-international?src=stats

Wang, L. L. (1988). Meritocracy and diversity in higher education: Discrimination against Asian Americans in the post-Bakke era. *The Urban Review, 20*(3), 189–209.

Wang, S., & Kim, B. S. K. (2010). Therapist multicultural competence, Asian participants' cultural values and counseling process. *Journal of Counseling Psychology, 57*(4), 394–401.

Wang, W. W., Chang, J. C., & Lew, J. W. (2009). Reasons for attending, expected obstacles, and degree aspirations of Asian Pacific American community college students. *Community College Journal of Research and Practice, 33*(7), 571–593.

Wei, M., Ku, T.-Y., & Liao, K. Y.-H. (2011). Minority status stress and college persistence attitudes among African American, Asian American, and Latino students: Perception of university environment as a mediator. *Cultural Diversity and Ethnic Minority Psychology, 11*, 195–203.

Western Interstate Commission for Higher Education (WICHE). (2012). *Knocking at the college door: Projections of high school graduates.* Boulder, CO: Author.

Wilton, L., & Constantine, M. G. (2003). Length of residence, cultural adjustment difficulties, and psychological distress symptoms in Asian and Latin American international college students. *Journal of College Counseling, 6,* 177–186.

Wing, Y. (1909). *My life in China and America.* New York, NY: Henry Holt and Company.

Wollenberg, C. M. (1978). *All deliberate speed: Segregation and exclusion in California schools, 1855–1975.* Berkeley: University of California Press.

Wong, A. (2013). Racial identity construction among Chinese American and Filipino American undergraduates. In S. D. Museus, D. C. Maramba, & R. T. Teranishi (Eds.), *The misrepresented minority: New insights on Asian Americans and Pacific Islanders, and the implications for higher education* (pp. 76–105). Sterling, VA: Stylus.

Wong, Y. J., Brownson, C., & Schwing, A. E. (2011). Risk and protective factors associated with Asian American students' suicidal ideation: A multicampus, national study. *Journal of College Student Development, 52*(4), 396–408.

Worthy, E. H., Jr. (1965). Yung Wing in America. *Pacific Historical Review, 34*(3), 265–287.

Wu, F. H. (2003). *Yellow: Race in America beyond Black and White.* New York, NY: Basic Books.

Wu, F. H., & Kidder, W. (2006). Asian Americans aren't White folks' "racial mascots." *Diverse: Issues in Higher Education, 23*(17), 48.

Yamamoto, J. K. (2011). *Aoki tells story of Japanese American Black Panther.* Retrieved from http://www.nikkeiwest.com/index.php/the-news/archived-article-list/93-aoki-tells-story -of-japanese-american-black-panther

Yang, R. K., Byers, S. R., Ahuna, L. M., & Castro, K. S. (2002). Asian-American students' use of a university student-affairs office. *College Student Journal, 36*(3), 448–470.

Yeh, T. L. (2002). Asian American college students who are educationally at risk. In M. K. McEwen, C. M. Kodama, A. N. Alvarez, S. Lee, & C. T. H. Liang (Eds.), *New Directions for Student Services: No. 97. Working with Asian American college students* (pp. 61–71). San Francisco, CA: Jossey-Bass.

Yeh, T. L. (2004). Issues of college persistence between Asian and Asian Pacific American students. *Journal of College Student Retention: Research, Theory and Practice, 6*(1), 81–96.

Yi, J. K., & Daniel, A. M. (2001). Substance use among Vietnamese American college students. *College Student Journal, 35*(1), 13–23.

Yoo, D. K. (2000). *Growing up Nisei: Race, generation, and culture among Japanese Americans of California, 1924–49.* Urbana: University of Illinois Press.

Yu, H. (2001). *Thinking orientals: Migration, contact, and exoticism in modern America.* New York, NY: Oxford University Press.

Yung Wing School P.S. 124. (2008). *Story of Yung Wing.* Retrieved from http://www .ps124.org/site_res_view_template.aspx?id=ea9776b6-61a6-44c3-9cbc-0ba7acc93df9

Zhang, W. (2013). Health disparities and relational well-being between multi- and monoethnic Asian Americans. *Social Indicators Research, 110*(2), 735–750.

Name Index

A

Abelmann, N., 5, 82
Abreo, A., 74
Ahn, A. J., 77
Ahuna, L. M., 100
Allen, W. R., 71
Al-Timmi, N., 103
Alvarez, A. N., 11, 73
Ancheta, A. N., 10, 13
Ancis, J. R., 3, 72
Andal, K. C. S., 33
Anderson, J. D., 18
Anderson, T. H., 49, 50
Andrews, M. M., 7, 12, 97
Aoki, A., 25
Asher, N., 25
Austin, A.W., 4, 38

B

Baker, A., 103
Balón, D. G., 81
Baron, A., 78
Behringer, L. B., 10
Bell, D. A., 9
Bok, D., 50
Bonilla-Silva, E., 28
Bonus, R., 23
Bow, L., 37
Bowen, W. G., 50
Brand, D., 22
Bresonis, K., 74

Brownson, C., 79
Bucceri, J. M., 78
Buenavista, T. L., 10, 23, 24
Byers, S. R., 100

C

Castro, K. S., 100
Chan, S., 15, 44, 53
Chang, E. S., 5, 70, 76, 88
Chang, J. C., 5, 70, 88
Chang, M. J., 5, 70, 76, 88
Chang, R. S., 9, 10, 104
Chang, T., 104
Chen, B., 75–76
Chen, C., 76
Chen, S., 78
Cheng, J. K. Y., 23, 24
Cheng, L. L., 27
Chew-Ogi, C., 25, 100
Chhuon, V., 73
Cho, E., 82, 84
Choi, Y., 23
Chu, J. P., 24
Chun, J., 7, 12, 97
Chung, C. Y., 57
Clarkberg, M. E., 72, 77
Clayton-Pedersen, A. R., 71
Cole, D., 87
Coloma, R. S., 98
Conner, K. R., 23
Constantine, M. G., 78, 103

Corbin, W., 80
Crenshaw, K., 9
Cress, C. M., 3, 79

D

Daniel, A. M., 80
Daniel, P. M., 19
Daniels, R., 4, 38
Davis, R. J., 96
DeLeon, J. M., 80
Delgado, R., 9–10
Diaz, V. M., 6
Douglass, J., 4
Draper, M., 78
Duberstein, P. R., 23
Dundes, L., 82, 84

E

Einarson, M. K., 72, 77
Esparrago, T., 23
Espenshade, T. J., 57, 61
Espiritu, A. F., 33
Espiritu, Y. L., 6, 7, 98
Ethington, C. A., 5

F

Fancher, T. L., 23
Fromme, K., 80

G

Garrod, A., 5
Gasman, M., 79, 82, 84, 91
George-Jackson, C. E., 12, 97
Gim Chung, R. H., 78
Gloria, A. M., 71, 72
Gonzalez, A., 82
Gorelick, S., 4
Gotanda, N., 9
Goto, S., 78
Goza, F., 28
Greenberger, E., 76
Grey, E. A., 10
Guyotte, R. L., 4, 33

H

Han, P. P., 25
Harper, S. R., 71

Hartlep, N. D., 98
Hayashino, D., 78
Heckhausen, J., 76
Heggins, W. J., 104
Helms, J. E., 73
Hing, B. O., 10
Hirano-Nakanishi, M., 45, 53
Ho, T. A., 71, 72
Hong, G. K., 75
Horn, R. A., 5
Hsia, J., 44, 53
Huang, C., 34
Huang, K., 78
Hudley, C., 73
Hune, S., 13, 15, 70, 71
Hurtado, S., 71
Hwang, W., 78
Hyun, J. K., 24

I

Ibrahim, F., 74, 75
Ignatiev, N., 8
Ikeda, E. K., 3, 79
Inkelas, K. K., 81, 104
Ito, L. A., 39
Iwamoto, D. K., 80

J

Jackson, J. F., 104
James, E. M., 34
James, T., 38
Johnson, A. B., 75
Johnson, L. B., 49–50
Johnston, M. P., 23
Joseph, P. E., 35, 41
Joshi, K. Y., 25

K

Kang, J., 57
Kao, G., 25
Karabel, J., 4
Kavanaugh, P. R., 103
Kawaguchi, S., 74
Kearney, L., 78
Khanna, N., 7
Kiang, P. N., 5, 70
Kibria, N., 74

Kidder, W. C., 3, 57–58
Kilkenny, R., 5
Kim, B. S. K., 77, 78
Kim, C. J., 21, 22, 73, 77
Kim, D., 82
Kim, E., 79
Kim, J. K., 73, 79, 84
Kim, W., 21, 104
Kisch, J., 79
Kodama, C. M., 11, 74
Ku, T.-Y., 79
Kurashige, S., 21
Kwak, S., 82, 84
Kwon, Y., 103

L

Laanan, F. S., 89
Ladson-Billings, G., 9
Lawrence, C., 9
Lee, C., 28
Lee, D., 79
Lee, E., 3, 15, 25, 28
Lee, J. J., 82
Lee, R. M., 27, 76–77
Lee, S. A., 11, 74, 81, 104
Lee, S. J., 25, 27, 77
Lee, S. S., 3–4, 56
Lei, J. L., 98
Leino, E. V., 79
Levine, D. O., 4
Levine, L., 103
Lew, J. W., 5, 25, 88
Liang, C. T. H., 11, 74, 81, 100
Liao K. Y.-H., 79
Lin, A. I., 78
Lin, M. H., 70
Literte, P. E., 7, 12
Liu, H. T., 76
Lloyd, K. D. J., 91
Loewen, J.W., 37, 38
Low, V., 31, 36
Lowe, S. M., 84
Lu, Y. E., 78
Lustig, S., 24
Ly, P., 24

M

Métraux, D. A., 15
Madon, T., 24
Major, E. M., 104
Mallinckrodt, B., 78
Maramba, D. C., 11, 14, 15, 23, 25, 70, 72–73, 74, 77, 91, 96
Matier, M. W., 72
Matsuda, M. J., 9, 10
McEwen, M. K., 11, 74, 75
McKinney, H., 24
Meekyung, H., 24
Milem, J. F., 71
Miville, M. L., 78
Mohr, J. J., 3
Moynihan, D. P., 19–20
Museus, S. D., 11, 25, 70, 72, 74, 81, 96, 104

N

Nadal, K. L., 15, 23, 74, 78
Nakanishi, D. T., 4, 45, 53, 70
Narui, M., 75
Ng, J. C., 3, 22, 56
Ngai, M. M., 40
Ngo, B., 25
Nishida, T. Y., 53

O

O'Brien, R. W., 4, 38, 39
Ogi, A. Y., 25, 100
Ohnishi, H., 74, 75
Okazaki, S., 12
Omatsu, G., 41
Okihiro, G. Y., 4, 38, 39
Omi, M., 8, 9, 14
Ong, A., 17, 25
Ono, K. A., 75
Orfield, G., 27, 28
Orsuwan, M., 5, 87
Osajima, K., 3
Otsuki, M., 80

P

Pak, Y. K., 3, 31
Palmer, R. T., 74, 91, 96

Pang, J. M., 25
Pang, V. O., 25, 27
Park, H. S., 104
Park, J. J., 10, 72, 77, 82, 88–89
Park, Y. S., 77
Parker, T. L., 10
Parrenas-Shimizu, C., 75
Peller, G., 9
Peng, S. S., 22
Pepin, S. C., 75
Pham, V., 75
Pituc, S. T., 23
Poon, O. A., 56, 70
Posadas, B. M., 4, 33
Poyrazli, S., 103

Q
Quinn, B. C., 24

R
Radford, A. W., 61
Ratanasen, M., 23
Reyes, A., 74
Rhoads, R. A., 82
Roediger, D. R., 8
Root, M. P. P., 7
Rorabaugh, W. J., 41
Rosenfeld, S., 40, 41, 42
Rudolph, F., 4
Ryabov, I., 28

S
Saad, C. S., 24
Sanaka, A., 103
Sandhu, D. S., 74, 75
Schwing, A. E., 79
Sedlacek, W. E., 3, 100
Shek, Y. L., 75, 81
Shibusawa, T., 78
Shigeoka, S., 78
Silverman, M. M., 79
Smith, T. D., 7
So, D. W., 80
Starobin, S. S., 89
Stefancic, J., 9, 10

Su, J., 77
Sue, D. W., 78
Sue, S., 24
Sullivan, N. Y., 78
Suzuki, B. H., 24, 78
Suzuki, L. A., 78
Synnott, M. G., 4

T
Takagi, D. Y., 4, 52, 53, 54, 55
Takaki, R., 9
Takeda, O., 25
Takemoto, M. A., 78
Takesue, K., 75
Takeuchi, D., 23
Talbot, D. M., 75
Tamura, E. H., 4, 31, 39
Tang, M., 82, 84
Tate, W. F., 9
Teranishi, R. T., 10, 11, 13, 14, 24, 29, 46, 50, 53, 70, 83, 87, 88–89, 96, 97
Thelin, J. R., 4
Thompson, J., 25
Ting, M. P., 81
Tochkov, K., 103
Torino, G. C., 78
Tseng, V., 83
Tuan, M., 14

U
Uba, L., 24
Umemoto, K., 42–43

V
Vang, S., 77

W
Wang, L. L., 44, 53
Wang, S., 78
Wang, W. W., 5
Wei, M., 79
Wilton, L., 103
Winant, H., 8, 9, 14
Wing, Y., 32

Wollenberg, C. M., 31, 35, 36, 37
Wong, A., 74
Wong, F. Y., 80
Wong, Y. J., 79
Worthy, E. H., Jr., 32
Wright, D., 22
Wu, D., 89
Wu, F. H., 3, 18, 21

Y

Yamada, M., 82

Yamamoto, J. K., 42
Yan Cheng, J. K., 24
Yang, R. K., 100
Yeh, T. I., 12, 70, 71
Yi, J. K., 80
Yoo, D. K., 39
Yoshida, E., 77
Yu, H., 33, 39, 40

Z

Zhang, W., 7

Subject Index

A

AALDEF. *See* Asian American Legal Defense and Education Fund (AALDEF)

AALF. *See* Asian American Legal Foundation (AALF)

AANAPISI. *See* Asian American and Native American Pacific Islander–Serving Institutions (AANAPISI)

AAPA. *See* Asian American Political Alliance (AAPA)

AAPI. *See* Asian American and Pacific Islander (AAPI)

Advancing Justice, 64–66

Affirmative action: in contemporary Asian America, 61–66; court cases on, 58–68; definition of, 49–51; late 20th century discourse of, 52–56; negative action *vs.*, 56–58; redefining merit, 52–56

Alexander v. Holmes County Board of Education (1969), 36

American citizenship, 18; Caucasian ancestry and, 8–9; Civil Rights Act and, 49–50; tenuous, 31–47

Aoki v. Deane (1907), 36–37

Asian, definition of, 6

Asian American: access to educational pipeline, 34–38; admissions scandals, 53–54, 55, 57; "civic ostracism," 21; definition of, 5–7; demands for equal representation in higher education, 40–47; "deminoritization" in higher education, 56; diversity of, 74–75; and educational pipeline, 31–47; as "nonminority" minorities, 4–5; race-conscious measures for, 14–15; as racial minorities in higher education, 13–15; research literature on race and, 8–11. *See also* Asian American identity; Model minority

Asian American and Native American Pacific Islander–Serving Institutions (AANAPISI), 5; descriptive data on, 93; emergence of, 88–93; grantees, 90; new designation of, 90–91; official designation of, 89–91

Asian American and Pacific Islanders (AAPIs), 1, 5; campus climate and, 70–73; categories, 6–7; college and career choices for, 82–85; college student experience of, 69–88; in community college, 85–88; conflation of, 101–105; disaggregation of data on, 96–97; educational attainment for, 26; enrollment in higher education, 53; enrollment in two- and four-year institutions, 51; family and intergenerational concerns, 76–78; growth of population, 16–17; and high school diploma, 29; identity development of, 73–76; leadership and involvement of, 81–82; mental health of, 78–81; multiracial, 97–98; participation in STEM, 96–97; population in the United States (1860–2050), 17; racial triangulation of, 21–22; risk factors for, 86

Asian American Center for Advancing Justice, 64

Asian American identity, 73; psychosocial development level of, 74; students' attitudes towards, 74

Asian American Identity Development Model, 73–74

Asian American Legal Defense and Education Fund (AALDEF), 65–66

Asian American Legal Foundation (AALF), 62–63, 66

Asian American Political Alliance (AAPA), 43

AsianCrit. *See* Critical Asian Theory (AsianCrit)

Asiatic barredzone Immigration Act, 16

B

Black Panther Party, 41, 43

Brown v. Board of Education (1954), 27, 36

C

Campus climate, 70–73; for Cambodian Americans, 73; for Filipino Americans, 72; perceptions of, 72–73; racial climate, 71–72

CEM. *See* Chinese Education Mission (CEM)

Central Asians, 7

Chinese Education Mission (CEM), 32

Chinese Exclusion Act, 15–16

"Civic ostracism," 21

Civil Rights Act of 1964, 18

Coalition of Bar Associations of Color, 63–64

Collective self-esteem, 79–80

College Cost Reduction and Access Act of 2007, 89

Community college, AAPIs in, 85–88, 98

Critical Asian Theory (AsianCrit), 9–11

Critical Race Theory (CRT), 9–11

CRT. *See* Critical Race Theory (CRT)

D

Depression and suicidal behavior, 79–80

"Dragon ladies," 75

E

East Asians, 7

Educational pipeline: access to, 34–38; *Aoki v. Deane* (1907), 36–37; Asian Americans and, 30–34; *Lum v. Rice* (1927), 37–38; *Tape v. Hurley* (1885), 35–36

Episodic drinking, 80

F

FAFSA. *See* Free Application for Federal Student Aid (FAFSA)

Filipino American identity, 77

Filipino Americans: community formation, 33–34; family and education environments, 77–78; and higher education, 24; identity of, 77; racial climates for, 72; *Roldan v. Los Angeles County* and, 9

Filipino Pensionado program, 32–33

Fisher v. University of Texas, 58, 59, 61, 67–68

Flatbush Boycott, 21–22

Free Application for Federal Student Aid (FAFSA), 84

Free Speech Movement (FSM), 40

FSM. *See* Free Speech Movement (FSM)

G

Gentlemen's Agreement, 16, 36

Global Organization of People of Indian Origin, 62

Gratz v. Bollinger (2003), 58–59

Grutter v. Bollinger (2003), 58, 59
Guam Community College, 92

H

Higher education: AAPI enrollment in, 53; Asian American exceptionalism in, 53–54; Blacks, Latinos, and AAPIs enrollment in, 46; Clark Kerr's Master Plan, 42–43; demands for equal representation in, 40–47; Free Speech Movement for, 40–41; as racial minorities in, 13–15; and segregation, 38–40
Hispanic National Bar Association, 63
House Un-American Activities Committee (HUAC), 41
Ho v. San Francisco Unified School District, 63
HUAC. *See* House Un-American Activities Committee (HUAC)

I

ICSA. *See* Intercollegiate Chinese for Social Action (ICSA)
Identity: of AAPIs, 73–76; Asian American, 73, 74; Filipino American, 77; pan-Asian American, 6, 31–32
Identity development, of AAPIs, 73–76
Immigration Act of 1924, 16
Immigration and Nationality Act of 1965, 16, 18, 52
Indian American Forum for Political Education, 62
Intercollegiate Chinese for Social Action (ICSA), 43

J

Japanese American Relocation Council (JARC), 38, 39
Japanese Americans: second-generation, 36–39; West Coast, 38; incarceration during World War II, 10; cultural resistance, 19

JARC. *See* Japanese American Relocation Council (JARC)
JEP. *See* Judicial Education Project (JEP)
Judicial Education Project (JEP), 62

K

K–12 education : Asian American students in, 24; 27–30; anti-Asian incidents and, 27; complexities of, 34; and court cases, 34–37; marginalization and, 37

L

Latina/o groups, 10
Los Angeles Riots, 21–22
Louis D. Brandeis Center for Human Rights under Law (LBD), 62
Lum v. Rice (1927), 37–38

M

MASC. *See* Mexican American Students Confederation (MASC)
McCarran–Walter Act, 16
Mental health, of AAPIs, 78–81; collective self-esteem, 73, 79–80; depression and suicidal behavior, 79–80; episodic drinking and, 80
Mexican American Students Confederation (MASC), 43
Model minority, 13–30; in legal system, 58–60; modern, 18–22; research beyond, 98; in school, 22–30; stereotype, 13

N

National Asian American Educational Foundation, 62
National Asian Pacific Bar Association, 63
National Bar Association, 63
National Defense Education Act (NDEA), 42
National Education Association (NEA), 28

National Federation of Indian American
Associations, 62
National Native American Bar Association,
63
National Science Foundation (NSF), 14,
97
Native Hawaiian and Pacific Islanders
(NHPI), 6
NEA. *See* National Education Association
(NEA)
Negative action: AALDEF and, 65; *vs.*
affirmative action, 56–58
*Negro Family: The Case for National Action,
The*, 19–20
New York Times Magazine, 18
NHPI. *See* Native Hawaiian and Pacific
Islanders (NHPI)
Nisei, 31, 36–39
Non-White populations: change, actual
and projected, 2; "minority" and
"majority" definition, 2

O

Open Doors Report, 101–103
Outsider racialization, 10, 13

P

PACE. *See* Philippine-American Collegiate
Endeavor (PACE)
Page Act, 15
Pan-Asian American identity, 6, 31–32
Parent–child conflict, 77–78
*Parents Involved in Community Schools v.
Seattle School District*, 27
Pew Research Center, 22
Philippine-American Collegiate Endeavor
(PACE), 43
Plessy v. Ferguson (1896), 36

R

Race: color and, 8; research literature on,
8–11; as social construction, 8–9
Racial discrimination, 2; AAPI admissions
and, 54–55; act against, 49–50;
entrenched structural, 19–20;

institutionalized, 49–50; perceived, 78,
79
Racial microaggression, 10, 78
Racial triangulation, of Asian Americans,
21–22
*Regents of the University of California v.
Bakke*, 4, 58–59
Roldan v. Los Angeles County, 9

S

San Francisco State College (SFSC), 42–44
*Schuette v. Coalition to Defend Affirmative
Action*, 67
SEAA. *See* Southeast Asian Americans
(SEAA)
Self-blame, 78
SFSC. *See* San Francisco State College
(SFSC)
South Asians, 7
Southeast Asian Americans (SEAA), 70;
academic struggles, 25; educational
access and attainment, 70; in South
Seattle Community College, 91
Southeast Asian and Pacific Islander
students: and high school diploma,
29–30; experiences in school, 25–27
Southeast Asians, 7
Stereotype: of model minority, 13, 51; of
yellow peril, 51
Sweatt v. Painter (1950), 60

T

Tape v. Hurley (1885), 35–36
Third World Liberation Front (TWLF),
43–44
TWLF. *See* Third World Liberation Front
(TWLF)

U

United States v. Bhagat Singh Thind, 9
U.S. News & World Report, 20, 102

W

West Asians, 7
Western Interstate Commission for Higher
Education (WICHE), 1

WHIAPPI. *See* White House Initiative on Asian Americans and Pacific Islanders (WHIAPPI)

White House Initiative on Asian Americans and Pacific Islanders (WHIAPPI), 88

WICHE. *See* Western Interstate Commission for Higher Education (WICHE)

Y

Yellow peril: new type of, 52; popularization of phrase, 15–17

About the Authors

Yoon K. Pak is an associate professor in education policy, organization, and leadership (EPOL), director of doctoral graduate programs for EPOL, and core faculty in Asian American studies at the University of Illinois at Urbana-Champaign. She is a past recipient of the National Academy of Education/Spencer Postdoctoral Fellowship and is a coeditor of the *History of Education Quarterly*. Her research and teaching interests focus on the history of American education in the 20th century as it relates to racial minorities and immigrant groups. She is also interested in contemporary higher education issues as it affects Asian American student populations. In addition to her book, *Wherever I Go I'll Always Be a Loyal American: Schooling Seattle's Japanese Americans During World War II*, she has also published in journals such as *Educational Theory, Review of Research in Education, Theory and Research in Social Education*, and *Urban Education*.

Dina C. Maramba is an associate professor of student affairs administration and affiliate faculty with Asian and Asian American studies at the State University of New York (SUNY) at Binghamton. With over 10 years of experience as a student affairs professional, among her many roles included working with first-generation students and facilitating their success in college. Her research focuses on equity, diversity, and social justice issues within the context of higher education. Her interests include how educational institutions and campus environments influence access and success among students of color, underserved, and first-generation college students. Her books include *The Other Students: Filipino Americans, Education and Power* (with Rick Bonus);

Fostering Success of Ethnic and Racial Minorities in STEM: The Role of Minority Serving Institutions (with Robert T. Palmer and Marybeth Gasman); and *The Misrepresented Minority: New Insights on Asian Americans and Pacific Islanders and Their Implications for Higher Education* (with Samuel Museus and Robert T. Teranishi). Her work includes publications in the *Journal of College Student Development*, *Journal of College Student Retention,* and *Research in Higher Education and Educational Policy.* Dr. Maramba is a recipient of the Award for Outstanding Contribution to Asian/Pacific Islander American Research in Higher Education by ACPA.

Xavier J. Hernandez is a PhD student in the Department of Education Policy, Organization, and Leadership at the University of Illinois at Urbana-Champaign. He received his MA degree in Asian American studies from San Francisco State University and his BA degree in criminology, law, & society from the University of California, Irvine. He has also studied abroad at the University of the Philippines, Diliman. His research interests include Asian American college preparation, access, and retention, with a particular focus on the influence of extracurricular involvement on Asian American educational experiences.

About the ASHE Higher Education Report Series

Since 1983, the ASHE (formerly ASHE-ERIC) Higher Education Report Series has been providing researchers, scholars, and practitioners with timely and substantive information on the critical issues facing higher education. Each monograph presents a definitive analysis of a higher education problem or issue, based on a thorough synthesis of signifi cant literature and institutional experiences. Topics range from planning to diversity and multiculturalism, to performance indicators, to curricular innovations. The mission of the Series is to link the best of higher education research and practice to inform decision making and policy. The reports connect conventional wisdom with research and are designed to help busy individuals keep up with the higher education literature. Authors are scholars and practitioners in the academic community. Each report includes an executive summary, review of the pertinent literature, descriptions of eff ective educational practices, and a summary of key issues to keep in mind to improve educational policies and practice.

The Series is one of the most peer reviewed in higher education. A National Advisory Board made up of ASHE members reviews proposals. A National Review Board of ASHE scholars and practitioners reviews completed manuscripts. Six monographs are published each year and they are approximately 144 pages in length. The reports are widely disseminated through Jossey-Bass and John Wiley & Sons, and they are available online to subscribing institutions through Wiley Online Library (http://wileyonlinelibrary.com).

Call for Proposals

The ASHE Higher Education Report Series is actively looking for proposals. We encourage you to contact one of the editors, Dr. Kelly Ward (kaward@wsu.edu) or Dr. Lisa Wolf-Wendel (lwolf@ku.edu), with your ideas.

ASHE HIGHER EDUCATION REPORT

ORDER FORM SUBSCRIPTION AND SINGLE ISSUES

DISCOUNTED BACK ISSUES:

Use this form to receive 20% off all back issues of *ASHE Higher Education Report*.
All single issues priced at **$23.20** (normally $29.00)

TITLE	ISSUE NO.	ISBN

Call 888-378-2537 or see mailing instructions below. When calling, mention the promotional code JBNND to receive your discount. For a complete list of issues, please visit www.josseybass.com/go/aehe

SUBSCRIPTIONS: (1 YEAR, 6 ISSUES)

☐ New Order   ☐ Renewal

U.S.	☐ Individual: $174	☐ Institutional: $327
CANADA/MEXICO	☐ Individual: $174	☐ Institutional: $387
ALL OTHERS	☐ Individual: $210	☐ Institutional: $438

Call 888-378-2537 or see mailing and pricing instructions below.
Online subscriptions are available at www.onlinelibrary.wiley.com

ORDER TOTALS:

Issue / Subscription Amount: $ _____

Shipping Amount: $ _____
(for single issues only – subscription prices include shipping)

Total Amount: $ _____

SHIPPING CHARGES:

First Item $6.00
Each Add'l Item $2.00

(No sales tax for U.S. subscriptions. Canadian residents, add GST for subscription orders. Individual rate subscriptions must be paid by personal check or credit card. Individual rate subscriptions may not be resold as library copies.)

BILLING & SHIPPING INFORMATION:

☐ **PAYMENT ENCLOSED:** *(U.S. check or money order only. All payments must be in U.S. dollars.)*

☐ **CREDIT CARD:**   ☐ VISA   ☐ MC   ☐ AMEX

Card number _____ Exp. Date _____

Card Holder Name _____ Card Issue # _____

Signature _____ Day Phone _____

☐ **BILL ME:** *(U.S. institutional orders only. Purchase order required.)*

Purchase order # _____
Federal Tax ID 13559302 • GST 89102-8052

Name _____

Address _____

Phone _____ E-mail _____

Copy or detach page and send to: **John Wiley & Sons, One Montgomery Street, Suite 1200, San Francisco, CA 94104-4594**

Order Form can also be faxed to: **888-481-2665**

PROMO JBNND